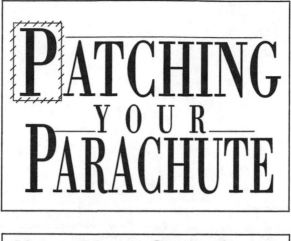

How You Can Beat Unemployment

DALE & SANDY LARSEN

INTERVARSITY PRESS
DOWNERS GROVE, ILLINOIS 60515

InterVarsity Press® is the book-publishing division of InterVarsity Christian Fellowship®, a student movement active on campus at hundreds of universities, colleges and schools of nursing in the United States of America, and a member movement of the International Fellowship of Evangelical Students. For information about local and regional activities, write Public Relations Dept., InterVarsity Christian Fellowship, 6400 Schroeder Rd., P.O. Box 7895, Madison, WI 53707-7895.

All Scripture quotations, unless otherwise indicated, are from the HOLY BIBLE, NEW INTERNATIONAL VERSION®. NIV®. Copyright ©1973, 1978, 1984 by International Bible Society. Used by permission of Zondervan Publishing House. All rights reserved.

Cover illustration: Roberta Polfus

ISBN 0-8308-1347-0

Printed in the United States of America ∞

Library of Congress Cataloging-in-Publication Data

Larsen, Dale.
    Patching your parachute: how you can beat unemployment/Dale &
Sandy Larsen.
        p.   cm.
    "Find work that matches your skills, meet family needs while
unemployed, reclaim emotional & spiritual control of your life."
    Includes bibliographical references.
    ISBN 0-8308-1347-0
    1. Unemployed—Psychology.   2. Unemployed—Life skills guides.
    3. Job hunting.   4. Unemployment—Psychological aspects.
    I. Larsen, Sandy.   II. Title.
    HD5708.L37   1993
    650.14—dc20   93-18097
                                                          CIP

17   16   15   14   13   12   11   10   9   8   7   6   5   4   3   2   1
07   06   05   04   03   02   01   00   99   98   97   96   95   94   93

Table of Contents

1

Not Just
A Victim

I went back to my desk, and I said to myself,
Do I cry or do I throw up?
Lillian, on being fired

I will take refuge in the shadow
of your wings until
the disaster has passed.
Psalm 57:1

t was December 7th. Pearl Harbor Day. It was a Thursday. All the big shots from the main office were there. The lunchroom was filled with people. This fat man with a beet-red face—he looked so embarrassed—he said very softly, 'We're closing down.' Half of us couldn't hear him. Everybody was whispering, 'What did he say?' He said it more loudly. Then he said, 'We could close right now, but we'll give you sixty days.' "

Lillian remembers the day in excruciating detail, just as a similar day is etched in each of our memories. It wasn't the comic-strip scene of Mr. Dithers shouting, "Bumstead, you're fired!" It was less dramatic than that—yet in another way more dramatic, because it was real.

Unlike Lillian, Robert doesn't remember the specifics of how he was told he wouldn't be rehired for his teaching job. But he does remember the frustration of not being able to find out why. He says, "I couldn't get a straight answer. The principal said he'd recommended that I be rehired, but the superintendent said the principal had recommended that I not be rehired. The most difficult part was not knowing."

Many Losses

For some, losing a job is a reality too painful to acknowledge. Robert Coulson tells of two executives who would not face the awful truth:

> One executive stumbled out of a Philadelphia office after being fired. Rather than face his family, the poor fellow caught a plane to Miami, where he went underground for two weeks until sheer boredom gave him the courage to tell his wife what had happened. She had been distraught. Another victim continued to commute to New York City from Westport, Connecticut, for the balance of his monthly commutation ticket, before admitting to his family that he had lost his job. Don't do that. Face the music.[1]

Joel had retired from one career and begun another when his wife's professional career moved them to a small college town. There he found himself abruptly unemployed—and apprehensive. He says, "Working is the only thing I've known since I was 13. I worked 38 years. Not working was uncharted territory. I didn't know how I'd react."

Why does unemployment hurt? The reasons are both obvious and complex. We need to work. For the money, yes, but not only for the money—for a sense of purpose and worth as well. "The fear of being fired touches a deep nerve. In our society, a person's job is crucial. When we lose our job, we lose our character, our essence. . . . We live in a free society, but most of us are afraid of being given our 'freedom.' "[2]

Of course most of us, while we're working, dream of not working. We fantasize about winning the lottery and going on permanent vacation. In reality, most big lottery winners stay on at their jobs, and some who quit later return to work.

The odds were 17 trillion to 1, but in October 1991 Don Wittman won his second $2 million lottery prize. Still he decided to stay on at his job as a carpenter. "Sure, I'm going to keep on working," he said. "Otherwise I'd just be bored."[3]

Judy Erpenbach quit her waitress job after she won $1,000 a week for life—but she went back to work part-time. She explained, "I was really bored, and I missed talking to all my customers. You need something to anchor your life. It makes it more real when you are working for some of your money."[4]

Work also makes us feel good about ourselves. No matter how we lost a job, we take it to mean we didn't measure up. The message is "You weren't good enough" no matter how the news is delivered—and often the news is not delivered graciously.

Most bosses do not like to fire people, and, what's worse, they often don't know how. "Nobody tells most executives how to do it. They are trained to interview, to hire, and to supervise, but hardly ever are they trained how to discharge. Moreover, nobody tells them what to do when *they* are fired."[5]

Greg was a computer technician whose company sold computer systems to the military. He knew that defense budget cutbacks were spelling trouble:

> I was called into the office and told "today's your last day." It was quite a shock. I knew the company was in bad shape but I figured I was pretty well "in." About a week later, they gave us three days of meetings to help us cope—mostly to help us write résumés. It was a very sorrowful meeting. People were crying. Other than those three days, I received no help coping with losing my job.

When Victor's department was cut back, he and several other long-time executives lost their jobs. He remembers the day clearly:

> There was no real warning. I was called into the chief exec-

utive's office. He informed me as gently as he could and offered severance pay. My first response was to ask for employment counseling instead. They also made it clear that I had no future anywhere in that company. Emotionally I was frozen—numb. However, I did believe it was happening. As I walked back to my desk, I entertained a few conspiracy theories of who wanted to get me out. I called my wife and told her right away. I didn't feel immediate resentment. The resentment came later, when good jobs were not forthcoming.

Losing a job hurts because the atmosphere of the job—the routine, the people, the rhythm of it all—is so woven into our life fabric. Lillian says: "I miss the people. It's like your family. A lot of them went to work at the new home-improvement store that opened, and I go out there to visit them. We're even having a store picnic, and our store doesn't exist anymore. Crazy, isn't it?"

Maybe not so crazy. Work is life. It defines us, structures our days, provides for our needs, gives us a reason to get up in the morning, brings us a sense of accomplishment. We gripe about it, but we need it and love it at the same time.

And now it's gone.

Grieving a Job Loss

First, you're numb. Did that really happen? Then you replay the conversation several times. Could I possibly have misunderstood? Then you get mad. How can they do this to me? Then you panic. What am I going to do?

You feel robbed, like a victim of a crime. Or chomped on, like the victim of a predator. If the position itself disappeared in a company reorganization, you probably feel run over by a giant impersonal machine. More precisely, you feel like an obsolete bolt no longer needed for the new model machine. No matter how well you performed, you no longer serve any function in the works and are destined for the scrap heap.

If you lost your job because of untrue rumors or because somebody lied about you—and yes, it does happen—you feel violated by injustice. You want a fair hearing. You want your rights. Maybe you want revenge.

If you were fired because your job performance didn't measure up, you feel regret and embarrassment and an intense desire to prove yourself again. "If only I'd tried harder . . ." "If only they'd give me a second chance . . ."

Maybe you were fired because you let your Christian values slip a little at the workplace. You let your desires control you. And you got caught. Now you feel guilty, ashamed, embarrassed. You feel you've failed God and let down the people who look up to you.

No matter what the reason, life is suddenly out of control. Sandwiched between the numbness of first hearing that you've lost your job and the later depression of despair are your emotions—a mixture of anger and fear.

You feel anger at the person who fired you, because of when and where it was said or how insensitively it was done. Anger at the place you work for, because you've given them your best and this is how they treat you. Anger at yourself for not measuring up, for not being good enough to keep your job. Anger at coworkers, known or anonymous, who may have spread bad reports about you. Anger at life in general for being so unfair. Even anger at God for jerking the rug out from under you. You've tried to serve him in your job, and you thought you could count on him. How could he let this happen?

Along with the anger is the attack of fear, which comes in a bombardment of panicky questions: "What are people going to think of me?" "How am I going to tell . . . (my marriage partner, my children, other people who are counting on me)?" "How am I going to pay my bills?" "Will I lose my house?" "Will I be out on the street?" And the biggest question of all: "Am I going to make it?" Not just financially (though that's a big enough question), but personally, emotionally, spiritually.

All those feelings start to boil while you're making your way back to the spot where you're supposed to finish out your day as a happy and productive employee. They say, "Thank you very much for your years of faithful service. Have a nice day." And you want to cry out with the psalmist:

Save me, O God,
for the waters have come up to my neck.
I sink in the miry depths,
where there is no foothold.
I have come into the deep waters;
the floods engulf me. (Psalm 69:1-2)

A few people do greet the loss of their job with "Whoopee!" They're unhappy where they work and they've longed for the chance to do something else, but they've never quite had the nerve to break free. Then there are the people in such high-demand occupations that if they lose one job, they have no trouble stepping into another one.

For the rest of us, which is most of us, losing a job is a terrible blow. All at the same time we feel victimized and feel it's all our fault. A big chunk of life which seemed safely predictable has been snatched from us, or we've dropped it.

Don't people realize that you need this job? Doesn't anybody understand that you had plans? You were counting on your work to provide for you and your family. You were looking ahead to a good future. Now you're scared to look forward. Instead of a job, you have a loss. Again, we cry out with the psalmist:

Answer me, O LORD, out of the goodness of your love;
in your great mercy turn to me.
Do not hide your face from your servant;
answer me quickly, for I am in trouble.
Come near and rescue me;
redeem me because of my foes. (Psalm 69:16-18)

How Bad Is It Really?

Or to put it more positively, what's potentially good about this radical change in your life?

The first advantage is one you may not have let yourself fully appreciate. Maybe for the first time in years, you don't have to get up and go to work in the morning. We're not being flippant. Being out of work has an immediate payoff: freedom. Your days become your own. Every morning you can decide for yourself what needs to be done, plus you have time to do it. Millions of securely employed people would kill (figuratively, anyway) for that privilege.

If you're anything like most of us, you've been unable to find the time to do half the things you want to do—and barely enough time to do what needs to be done. Suddenly your hours are yours. Suddenly nobody's your boss but you. Haven't you dreamed of days like this? Now, for a while at least (until the financial pinch sets in), why not let yourself enjoy the luxury?

People who have functioned well in rigidly structured jobs may find the new freedom difficult. They don't know what to do with themselves when nobody's telling them what to do. If you're like that, then the sudden free time is harder for you to handle, but it can surprise you with how profitable it becomes. You'll wind up discovering interests and abilities you didn't know you had.

That brings us to a second advantage of this sudden disruption of your regular life: you finally have the opportunity to make some of the changes you always wished you could make.

Now is the ideal time to make an honest evaluation of your old job. Did you really love it as much as you claimed at class reunions? Did you really hate it as much as you complained to your spouse? What (if anything) made it meaningful or challenging or stimulating or fun? How did it cramp your gifts and abilities? What were the things about your job that drove you crazy?

This is more than a "sour grapes exercise." We're not suggesting you throw darts at a picture of your old boss. We are suggesting that if there are things about your old job that left you dissatisfied, now is the perfect time to make a change. (In chapter five we'll explore that question more fully.)

Most of us would say we don't like being in situations which are out of our control. But doesn't much of the fun in life come from deliberately doing exactly that: engaging ourselves with forces beyond our control and playing with them? Sports are an obvious example. It's the lack of control over the opponent which puts the challenge and meaning into any sport.

In 1992 the Pittsburgh Pirates were a breath away from the National League pennant when in the ninth inning they found they couldn't control the Atlanta Braves, and a score of 0-2 turned into 3-2. That's what sports are all about.

Who wants to watch a 44-0 football game, even if your team is the winner? The same principle works when the "other side" is natural forces, as in sailing or mountain climbing. Whether pushing off from the top of a ski hill, stepping into the batter's box, or sitting down at a chess board, the fun comes from playing with forces that seem bigger than we are.

In unemployment as in sports, the most important factor within your control is your attitude. In the first shock of unemployment, "attitude" may be confused with "feelings" and may be lousy. But attitude means a decision of the mind, which includes deciding how we're going to feel—or more precisely deciding which feelings will be allowed to dominate our thinking.

What Difference Does It Make?
Does it make any difference to be a Christian at a time like this? That question matters a great deal.

If you're a Christian who is unemployed—or if you think you might be shortly—or if you know and care about someone who is—then it's an absolutely crucial question. It's crucial because Christians live and work in this world where all kinds of bad things happen, including losing our jobs.

Our presence in this unkind world system is no accident. Christ has deliberately put us here. "As you sent me into the world, I have sent them into the world" (John 17:18). Christians are subject to the same economic forces, the same business fluctuations, the same personality clashes as the rest of the population. Our beliefs are no insulation against an uncertain economy, and our faith is no guarantee that we will always have a cushy job. We live and work and sometimes become unemployed just as other people do.

Think how many synonyms we have in our language for "getting fired": "get the boot," "get the sack," "get canned," "be dismissed," "be discharged"—and the latest and most coldly mechanistic, "be terminated." People have been losing their jobs since Adam was "dismissed" by God from tending the Garden of Eden. As long as people have been working for anybody besides themselves, people have been getting fired. So being unemployed is an occasional part of being human. But a Christian can experience unemployment and the search for work in a unique way not shared by the rest of the world.

How? First, even in this bad situation of unemployment, when we feel so victimized, as Christians we have a unique hope. Christian hope is not wishful thinking ("if I sit around and dream long enough, God will bring the perfect job my way"). It is not magic ("if I believe hard enough, the first interview I have will be successful"). Our unique hope is based not on the nation's economics or our job skills, but on the fact that a living, personal, redeeming God is involved with our lives and cares about what's happening to us.

Our hope is that the God we know and serve, and who lives in us, will redeem the worst situation and bring good out of it. That's the essence of the much-quoted verse Romans 8:28—

"And we know that in all things God works for the good of those who love him." That verse is in the context of a long passage about living in the Holy Spirit and suffering and how God works through pain to make us more like Christ. Unfortunately, Romans 8:28 is sometimes thrown at depressed people with the expectation that they should cheer up right away. The promise was never meant as an instant cure for unhappy feelings or a guarantee of finding a job in an hour. It is a promise of hope which those who don't love God cannot claim.

The promise is realistic. It admits that the situation is bad, but it says the Lord will work in this situation and bring good out of it. Nobody but God knows at this point what that "good" is or will be. We may know someday, looking back, or we may never know exactly, because we do not have God's perspective and knowledge. But we can be confident that God is a redeeming God, and that this way of drawing good out of bad is the strange and (to us) illogical way God works.

There's another assurance which belongs to unemployed Christians: We will not have to resort to underhanded means to survive. We have God's promise (though we may not feel it now) that our needs—for work, for sufficient finances, for meaning, for a sense of worth—will be met one way or another.

From prison Paul wrote to thank some distant friends for their generous gift, and then he assured them that "my God will meet all your needs according to his glorious riches in Christ Jesus" (Philippians 4:19). Christians through history have taken that promise and personalized it for themselves.

The promise does not say "how" or "when," but it does say that meeting our needs is God's will and pleasure. Scripture is full of promises which say much the same. It may happen in unexpected ways (in fact it probably will; it seems that whenever we try to predict how God will do something, he delights in surprising us). The point is that because God cares, we will survive, and it will not be necessary to disobey God in order to survive.

An unemployed Christian is not a helpless victim. Write that on your mirror, your refrigerator, the dashboard of your car. God is with you in this. You may not have a job or any immediate prospects for a job, but you have the certainty that you belong to a living God who created you for his own good purpose and who cares for you.

By "certainty" we don't mean "emotional assurance." That's a feeling; it will come and go. By "certainty" we mean "objective fact." The truth in the real world is that God does live in you if you're a believer. God does care. God does act on your behalf. God does inspire your thinking if you let him. God does empower you to take the right actions within his will. God also sends just the right encouragement at the right time.

Things to Do

☐ Make notes of everything good about your new situation, no matter how trivial they sound.

☐ Begin evaluating your old job. What did you like and dislike about it?

☐ Tell God exactly how you feel about your life.

☐ Resolve not to cut yourself off from prayer, Bible study and Christian fellowship.

Suggested Reading

Coulson, Robert. *The Termination Handbook.* New York, N.Y.: The Free Press, 1981. Written by an attorney, "a book for those on both sides of the 'firing line' "—the employer and the employee.

Maurer, Harry. *Not Working: An Oral History of the Unemployed.* New York, N.Y.: Holt, Rinehart & Winston, 1979. Interviews with unemployed people nationwide, in a style imitative of Studs Terkel's books, such as *Working.*

Leventman, Paula Goldman. *Professionals out of Work.* New York, N.Y.: The Free Press, 1981. A sympathetic study of Bos-

ton-area professional people who found themselves jobless.
Tarrant, John J. *Getting Fired: An American Ordeal.* New York,
N.Y.: Van Nostrand Reinhold Company, 1974. Tarrant set out
to write a "how to" book for getting a job after being fired
and got "emotionally involved with the subject matter."

2

Getting Unstuck: Reclaiming Control

I keep saying, "I know I'll get out and look for a job.
I know I will." But when?
Kyle, describing his times of unemployment

I sought the LORD,
and he answered me;
he delivered me from all my fears.
Psalm 34:4

For fifteen years Lyn worked at the same store. Her job seemed secure. She was counting the years till retirement. Then in one crushing jolt she and all her coworkers were told that the store was closing. To all appearances, Lyn immediately got very busy looking for another job.

I got applications from everywhere and filled them in. I went around asking people if I could use them for references. I filled out all the forms. But I've still got them all stashed in my bedroom. I never turned any of them in.

After the store closed, people in Lyn's church would come up to her and assure her they were praying for her. As the weeks wore on, their comments changed to "Don't you have a job yet?" or "Aren't you tired of living on unemployment?"

Lyn blames unemployment benefits for her lack of action. "If they hadn't given us that money," she says, "I'd have had to go out and get a job right away." Yet she seems stalled by something deeper than the convenience of an unemployment check.

Kyle has known several times of unemployment in his life. Even when he's short of money and (as he puts it) "avoiding the landlady," he puts off applying for jobs. He calls it a simple failure of nerve. "When you're unemployed is the time when you need the most courage and confidence," he says, "but that's when you have the least."

"They just don't want to work." The words come easily to our lips when somebody who's out of work doesn't appear to be doing anything about it. Kyle suggests another possibility: "It isn't that people don't want to work. What they really don't want is to go through the process of rejection."

Phil agrees. Now a self-employed painter, he was doing sales work when his company told him he was no longer needed. He says: "I think especially for guys, job-hunting can be a devastating experience. It isn't that you can't go out and look for a job, it's that you can't handle the rejection. Being told no over and over is more than you can handle."

Those who have been furthest up the corporate structure, those least accustomed to rejection, may have the hardest time getting unstuck. In her study of Boston professionals who lost their jobs in the 1970s, Paula Leventman wrote:

Well-placed scientists, engineers, and data analysts were stunned, literally shocked, to find themselves suddenly out of work. Virtually all initially experienced job loss as "traumatic" or "ego shattering." The pain of the event was so intense that detailed descriptions were often difficult to elicit. As time went on, loss of accustomed work routine, loss of the economic function, loss of the ability to provide for one's family, and repeated experiences of rejection resulted in erosion of self-confidence and in psychic disorientation. Unemployment was not an experience any were prepared to cope with.[1]

Who wants to be rejected? Nobody. We may start out with a

bang looking for a job. But as time wears on and the rejections mount up, inertia sets in. Curtis, an aspiring artist, describes it like this: "Time creates more and more frustration. Early on, you follow through on job leads, but then you start to get frustrated. It gets harder to get dressed up and go out and do it. You start to assume you won't get the job anyway."

Despite what Phil said about men and rejection, Lyn demonstrates that the same fear belongs to women. The unemployment check on which she depended has run out, and she can no longer afford health insurance—yet still she procrastinates.

The months have given Lyn new perspective on herself. "It's the fear of starting over," she now says. "I felt secure at my old job. I know I'm going to have to make up my mind to do something about the situation, but I keep saying, 'Next week, next week I'll get a job.' "

Stuck. Maybe that's the best word for it.

Getting in Gear

How does an unemployed person who is "stuck" get unstuck?

We can set the alarm clock ever earlier and make ever longer lists of places to go and things to do, but the real answer lies in the emotions and in the spirit, because that's where the problem is. That's where we tell ourselves, "I just can't do it today."

While financial expenditures may seem most pressing, it's just as important to count up our emotional and spiritual "expenditures." What is the experience of unemployment "costing" us emotionally? What resources do we have to meet that cost?

Phil found odd jobs to do after he lost his sales job. As he puts it, "I'm the kind of person that between somebody asking me if I could do something and my going and doing it, I would figure out how to do it." He had ways to cope financially, but he was immobilized by his own sense of worthlessness: "My vivid recollection is not so much being unemployed, but the low feeling of having no worth. It's a feeling of 'Nobody needs me. I'm not worth anything to anybody. If I had worth, somebody would hire me.' "

To this day Victor knows there was nothing he could have done to save his job. He lost his executive position when his department was cut back. Yet to this day, like most of the people we interviewed for this book, he blames himself.

I'd take the dog for walks at night, and some of those walks got very long. I'd sit down on a bench and ask God, "What did I do wrong? Why are you punishing me? When are you going to pick me up?" I don't remember being angry at God. I felt it was all my fault, that I had failed, that I had loused up, that I wasn't good enough. I couldn't make myself sufficiently important there to keep my job.

That's in the face of the fact that the loss of a job is often not the worker's fault at all.

In most cases, people are fired for reasons that have little to do with their own work: It was the wrong job; business was bad; somebody didn't like them; management changed; the company was reorganized. Don't take it personally unless there is no other explanation. Life goes on.[2]

While we Americans often define ourselves by our work, the emotional hurt and frustration of being unemployed are not uniquely American. John E. I. Ogar, a Nigerian Christian, describes his own struggles at not being able to find work: "More than two years ago, when I was newly graduated from the university, my prospects appeared bright and I had tall ambitions. I believed that I would be launched into a posh career within a few months. But the months have dragged on and on, and I am still unemployed!

"Unemployment can open the floodgates of frustration, depression, doubt, deprivation and despair. When I see my peers advancing in the world while I stagnate, unable to execute my well-laid plans, I feel frustrated." John confesses he asks himself, "Does God really care for me? Does he love me? Is he alive?"[3]

Twenty years ago Tim Hansel had his life all figured out and meticulously planned: "When I became a Christian at Stanford, I had strong, neat, crisp images of what my future was going to be like. I was going to be physically strong . . . intellectually acute . . . emotionally bomb-proof—and spiritually profound."

Tim's perfect world was literally crushed in a fall from a snow bridge while mountain-climbing. His injuries brought on deteriorating arthritis which left him in lifelong pain. It was the opposite of the life Tim had imagined for himself. He concluded: "I had a choice. I knew by now that the damage was permanent, that pain would be a companion for the rest of my journey. I had to learn a whole new way of living or fold up my cards. The deck was stacked. The life I'd always known was never to be again."[4] Tim came to accept his physical disability; he chose not to accept despair.

The happy fact is that not all unemployed people get stuck. Some are able to pick themselves up promptly and go on, like Robert, who was not rehired for his teaching job. He describes himself as "kind of an opportunist":

> I didn't spend too much time worrying about it. Teaching wasn't the only thing I could do. In times of change I try to look at it as an opportunity to see what's coming next. At first I looked for other teaching jobs in the area. I'd been doing some landscaping on the side ever since college, and we looked for a place to go into that full-time.

Landscaping met Robert's family's needs for a time, but it was very seasonal, and he eventually moved into other work. Still, he says strongly: "Just doing, taking action, starting on something that meets some of our needs, is important. It also looks better to a prospective employer."

Greg tried to keep "just doing" when he lost his highly skilled computer technician job through government cutbacks. He says, "I never felt angry. There should always be a different angle if one thing doesn't work out. You have to make up your mind to take whatever is available. There is always some way to make it—though it may not pay what you're used to."

Some abruptly unemployed people are able to do that and to go on. But others find themselves mired in a long period of non-action. "You feel sorry for yourself," recalls Victor, the one who lost an executive position after more than ten years. "At first I didn't pursue other jobs because I just didn't have the energy to sit down and organize things. I was so low."

"I started watching too much TV," is what Kyle remembers. He continues:

It was easy because it was passive. You sit there and you don't have to do anything. Of course then your self-esteem goes down even further, because what kind of person are you if all you do is sit and watch TV?

Yet I was also angry, usually at myself, but I would direct it at the people around me. I'd be mad—that I quit a job without having something else lined up; that I didn't like most of the jobs I was applying for; that I was supposed to "have all this potential" and I wasn't using it. I was even mad that a person has to go out and get a job, that you don't just wake up with one.

Victor eventually went into business for himself and is doing well financially. He admits, however, that he is still emotionally "stuck." His business, he says, "keeps him occupied," but he is still struggling with the hurt, now more than a decade old, of that day when his job vanished.

Problem-Solving

In 1980 the authors were at an especially "stuck" period in our work lives and in other ways. Dale was looking for a job as a Christian-education director in a church, and Sandy was working temporary secretarial jobs waiting for that magic day when

Dale's full-time church job would free her to write. The months were wearing on, and we weren't finding the solution we craved.

On one of her temporary jobs, Sandy picked up a scientific journal and read an article on creative problem-solving. It made these arresting statements:

If you are getting nowhere on a problem, abandon your approach and try to find a new difficulty as a basis for solving the problem. . . . Good reasoners do not persist in one direction if they are getting nowhere. . . . Poor reasoners, on the other hand, persist doggedly in the same direction, even when the difficulty does not yield to their efforts.

In other words, we get stuck when we get locked into looking at a problem one way and stubbornly pursuing one solution. That goes for job-hunting as well as scientific inquiry. We were locked into "a staff position at a church" as *the* solution to our employment problem, and it wasn't working. The article above gave several "precepts" for bumping our thinking out of the single-solution rut:

☐ Produce a second solution after the first. (Seems obvious, but we hadn't done that.)

☐ Critically evaluate your own ideas. Constructively evaluate the ideas of others. (That's hard when we're sure we're right, but look for strong points in others' advice and weak points in our own.)

☐ When stuck, change your representational system. If a concrete representation isn't working, try an abstract one, and vice versa. (At this and several other decision points in our marriage, we've made a "branch" chart of possible courses of action and possible results. It's a refreshing change from working things through verbally.)

☐ Take a break when you are stuck. (The job problem easily becomes the topic husbands and wives talk about all the time. Know when enough is enough.)

☐ Talk about the problem with someone. (Talking is exactly what many unemployed people are reluctant to do. Do it, but be selective. While it helps to tell as many people as possible that we're looking for work, it's not prudent to spread abroad our emotional problems coping with unemployment. Notice it says "someone" not "everyone.")[5]

Of the people we talked with who were unemployed or had gone through times of unemployment, those who found it hardest to get unstuck were people who had old resentments and scars, either from their previous jobs or from other happenings. They were continuing to expend their energy in anger rather than getting on with life.

Take an Emotional Inventory

Our friend Joel retired from the military, held an office job for several years, then took retirement from that. He took another office job briefly before his wife got a professional position in another state, where they moved. Joel expected to promptly find other work there, but he was disappointed to find that a small town had little to offer.

Joel puts it in somewhat military terms: "You need to count up your stress factors, determine what they are, fall back and regroup as much as possible before going out to apply for other jobs." In his own situation Joel identified these stress factors:

☐ a cross-country move
☐ wife's job change
☐ retirement (twice)
☐ new job only six months before the move

Those were on top of not being able to find work despite credentials in a number of professional positions as well as a military career.

The point is, we don't face unemployment in a vacuum. When you're feeling stuck and can't walk out the door to make another job application, take an emotional inventory. Find out what emotional roadblocks need to be understood and cleared away or hurdled so you can get on with life.

Have you ever seen the "Holmes and Rahe Social Readjustment Rating Scale"? The chart, developed in 1967 by Thomas H. Holmes and Richard H. Rahe, assigns point values to 43 different stress-causing events with a maximum of 100 points per event. Holmes and Rahe believed that point totals for recent events could help predict a person's chance of serious illness in the following two years.

Here's how several work-related items score on the Holmes-Rahe scale: "Dismissal from work" scores 47 points; "Business readjustment" scores 39; "Change in financial status" racks up 38 points; "Change to different line of work" counts for 36; "Change in work responsibilities" counts for 29; "Trouble with boss" earns you 23 points; and "Change in work hours, conditions" adds 20. That's 232 points toward getting sick just from losing your job.

The events on the Holmes-Rahe scale are acute stress factors. Some people we talked to were also weighed down by long-term stress factors (such as a poor relationship with a parent or other family member, or chronically thinking poorly of themselves) which surfaced again and affected their response to unemployment. If we still hear an angry authority figure shouting, "You're no good, you'll never amount to anything!" we'll be at a major disadvantage selling ourselves to a prospective employer.

Take a Spiritual Inventory

Our faith can turn a period of unemployment into a blessing by prodding us to face unresolved problems in our spiritual lives. In his book *The Sensation of Being Somebody*, Maurice Wagner gives a fuller picture of why Christianity is such a help to the jobless. All of us, he says, develop false "equations" to verify ourselves, such as:

Appearance + Admiration = a Whole Person

Performance + Accomplishments = a Whole Person

Status + Recognition = a Whole Person

When we stop trying to qualify for God's love and accept his unconditional salvation, says Wagner, we "find a new equation for our sense of being somebody, and this one truly balances. It is God + Me = a Whole Person."[6]

It's easy to see how we can depend on work to fill the left side of those equations. When the work disappears, the equation falls apart. But it's bound to fall apart anyway. Such equations are inherently unstable because they are based on fluid circumstances rather than on our relationship with an unchanging God, "who does not change like shifting shadows" (James 1:17).

In Christ we find the security to survive no matter what the world may throw at us—including those inevitable job-hunting rejections. Through Christ it's possible to "approach your job search from a less ego-involved perspective."[7] That doesn't mean a non-ego-involved perspective; after all, we're talking about going out and selling ourselves as the best person for the job. That takes ego strength! But our ego does not have to be involved in such a life-and-death way that rejection demolishes us.

When Harry Maurer interviewed hundreds of unemployed Americans for his book *Not Working*, he was surprised at the comfort which evangelical Christians drew from their faith. From his secular viewpoint, he analyzed it this way:

I was surprised by the number of unemployed who said that religion—usually some form of born-again Christianity—was their source of strength. One reason is that their belief in a benign Being makes them feel less alone—and unemployment can be a very lonely ordeal. They also feel sure that passionate faith will bring good things in its wake, that God will provide. . . . Equally important is the sense that whatever happens, it is probably for the best. To the evangelical Christian, unemployment may be confusing and painful, but at least it is not a meaningless disaster since the Lord presumably has his reasons. And in any case, it is not this world, with its tribulations, that matters, but the next.[8]

With a Little Help

Talking to other people can also help us get unstuck. Unfortunately, the temptation is to withdraw into ourselves, shutting out any risk of further hurt. At church, people may be too polite or too embarrassed to ask us about our job loss. Or they may not know—though we think it's written all over us. Hard as it is, we'll probably have to take the initiative to share our problem.

When Victor was asked how he coped with people knowing he was out of work, he replied simply, "Nobody asked about it." If you find that people you know are acting like they don't care, perhaps they don't know. Or perhaps they assume you don't want to talk about it.

We were fascinated to find that (unlike Leventman and Maurer's experience of not being able to get people to talk) nearly all the people we interviewed had a great compulsion to talk about their unemployment. Once they started, we barely needed to ask any questions. For some, the experience of unemployment was a few years past, and they had had time to resolve some things. Or is it possible that at first people don't want to talk about it at all because of their anger, hurt, embarrassment—so they don't talk—and then later nobody asks about it, so the chance never comes?

Cutting off your family from this difficult part of your life will only make things more difficult for them as well as you. Robert found that his time of unemployment was "a time of strengthening family commitment to each other as we tried to get through this time together."

Norm credits his wife, Sylvia, with "dealing with all of this remarkably well. She'd say, 'I believe in you,' or 'We'll make it' or point out how the Lord was providing for us. I haven't always been able to talk to her about all this because I haven't known what my emotions were or how to say it. My fears that have no name or description."

Unfortunately, not all families are helpful. Kyle recalls: "It seems my family judges you by whether you have a job. Like suddenly I become less than their relative because I'm not working. It becomes *the* topic of conversation—'Have you found anything yet? Are you looking?' When a person needs encouragement the most is when my family gives it to you the least."

The church family can also be a valuable support, especially if you have been feeling rejected by God or angry with him. God often chooses to express his love and care for us through other people. Other Christians' spiritual support and physical presence can be an answer to your question "Where is God when I need him?" Paul wrote:

> Praise be to the God and Father of our Lord Jesus Christ, the Father of compassion and the God of all comfort, who comforts us in all our troubles, so that we can comfort those in any trouble with the comfort we ourselves have received from God. For just as the sufferings of Christ flow over into our lives, so also through Christ our comfort overflows. (2 Corinthians 1:3-5)

Of course some churches do better at comfort than others. Some groups of Christians are very sensitive to hurts in their midst and respond compassionately. Others either don't notice or, steeped in rugged individualism, think it's none of their business to interfere with someone's personal problems. But even if your church is generally not a fellowship which responds readily to need, in any church there are a few people who have the gift of seeing and helping. Often they are the people who have been through it themselves. As the Scripture above says, once we have been comforted by God, we are better equipped to comfort others in the same way.

Norm found the voice of God in the ministry of others when he "came as close to a nervous breakdown as I've ever come."

I was angry with God, and that's a problem because you're "not supposed" to be angry with God—he's perfect. I called U-Haul and was going to sell our furniture and leave. Sylvia called our pastor, and he called back and invited us to a prayer meeting that Wednesday night. We went, but I went ready to attack the pastor and cut down everything he said. He came right out and told the people, "Norm has really struggled with something. He puts all of himself into things and when it fails it is devastating to him."

That man disarmed my hurt by entering into my anger. How are you going to jump on somebody that's on your side of the fence?

Six elders prayed for me, and they all started weeping. I asked the pastor, "What should I do?" He said "Nothing—it's up to us to bring you through." They ministered to that little boy inside who was always crying for somebody to say he was okay.

Afterward, I don't think I got a job particularly fast or anything like that, but I found I could cope with life. God has shown me that I don't understand his love, but he's told me to rest in it.

When you find yourself stuck, become healthily curious about why. The Holmes-Rahe Scale, while not sacred, may help identify and explain some of the immediate stresses weighing on you. If you find longer-term resentments or pains resurfacing, find someone you can talk to who can help you work your way free. It may be your pastor or elders, as in Norm's case, or it may be some other spiritually mature person you trust. Above all, it needs to be someone you trust and who is trustworthy.

Things to Do
☐ Have a family conference.
☐ Take an emotional inventory.
☐ Begin establishing a personal support network.

Suggested Reading

Figler, Howard. *The Complete Job-Search Handbook: All the Skills You Need to Get Any Job and Have a Good Time Doing It.* Rev. ed. New York, N.Y.: Henry Holt & Co., 1988. A book about developing specific job-finding skills: "self-assessment," "detective," "communication" and "selling yourself."

Hansel, Tim. *You Gotta Keep Dancin'.* Elgin, Ill.: David C. Cook Publishing, 1985. Hansel's honest and unsentimental account of how he chooses God's joy in the midst of constant pain. Also available as study kit with tape and leader's guide.

Holmes, Thomas H., and Richard H. Rahe. "Social Readjustment Rating Scale." *Journal of Psychosomatic Research* 2(1967), pp. 213-18. Reprinted with some updating in Helen K. Hosier, *Suddenly Unemployed,* San Bernardino, Calif.: Here's Life Publishers, Inc., 1992, p. 52.

Hyman, Ray, and Barry Anderson. "Solve It." *Chemtech,* May 1980, pp. 275-79. Originally published in *International Science and Technology.*

Krannich, Ronald L. *Careering and Re-careering for the 1990s.* Manassas, Va.: Impact Publications, 1989. Treats today's economic turbulence as an opportunity instead of a threat.

Wagner, Maurice. *The Sensation of Being Somebody.* Grand Rapids, Mich.: Zondervan, 1975. This Christian psychologist's premise is that we need a sense of belonging, worth and competence, and that we receive these from knowing God.

3

Buying Time

*And my God will meet all your needs
according to his glorious riches in Christ Jesus.*
Philippians 4:19

osing a job fills us with an awful sense of powerlessness: "What can I do?" The instinctive answer is "nothing." But that isn't true. There are plenty of things we can do. We just need time to do them before the wolf arrives at the door and the creditors come knocking and discouragement gets the upper hand.

Don't Stop Giving
The first answer may be surprising. It is "Don't stop being generous."

Phil and his family have coped with his erratic employment partly by staying generous. Phil says, "Frankly, I don't know how we've coped financially. But we have. It takes a lot of prayer. We try to give a lot. Giving has been a big part of our lifestyle." They added a small apartment over their garage and often have people staying there who have no place else to go.

No matter what their financial status, they are always ready to try to help somebody in need. This keeps them from being self-centered and reminds them of how well off they really are.

The Christian paradox, the liberty of knowing a God who owns "the cattle on a thousand hills" (Psalm 50:10), is that we can continue giving to others even when we feel we don't have much. When Paul wrote to the Corinthian Christians reminding them of a gift they had promised to give, he encouraged their generosity by telling them about the Macedonians who, out of "their overflowing joy and their extreme poverty . . . gave as much as they were able, and even beyond their ability" (2 Corinthians 8:2-3). Paul continued:

> And God is able to make all grace abound to you, so that in all things at all times, having all that you need, you will abound in every good work. As it is written: "He has scattered abroad his gifts to the poor; his righteousness endures forever." Now he who supplies seed to the sower and bread for food will also supply and increase your store of seed and will enlarge the harvest of your righteousness. You will be made rich in every way so that you can be generous on every occasion, and through us your generosity will result in thanksgiving to God. (2 Corinthians 9:8-11)

Paul's point was not that giving is a way for us to manipulate God and become rich, "but that there might be equality" (2 Corinthians 8:13) and God will be praised.

Spend Less

While we're staying generous, at the same time wisdom leads us to start spending less on ourselves.

Really? The normal response to that advice is either (a) "Yeah, that's easy for you to say," or (b) "No fun!" Either way, we can't escape the truth that being unemployed means we have to spend less because we have less to spend. Cleverly disguised in that ugly fact is a liberating potential—the discov-

ery that "living well" is as much in the mind and will as in the
physical aspects of life.

Have you noticed how some people, suddenly on a reduced
budget, adopt a "poor me" attitude? Every dollar saved is a cer-
tificate of martyrdom. Every purchase forgone merits a medal
for self-denial. For such people, thrift feels like forced servi-
tude. Why? Because they feel they've lost control over an in-
tensely personal and important part of life—their money.

In the authors' situation, our income is completely erratic
and sometimes nonexistent for weeks at a time. No matter what
the circumstances, each week the two of us get together with
paper and pencil to decide how much we need for food, gas-
oline, possible repairs on the house, the week's bills and other
weekly expenses plus a little extra for the unexpected. Then we
decide how much we can deposit or need to withdraw from our
account, and (if necessary) what will be paid now and what will
have to wait.

We have also decided to live well no matter what our income.
Deciding to live well within the money available puts power
back into our hands. Here's a chance for the unemployed family to work together instead of fighting over how much can't be
spent for what. "Better a dry crust with peace and quiet than
a house full of feasting, with strife" (Proverbs 17:1). With the
spending initiative back in our court, a restricted budget becomes not a matter of "Don't spend this, we can't buy that," but
rather, "Where will we, together, choose to use this money the
smartest and best?"

That job becomes more difficult when there are teenage children in the family who are bombarded with all the pressures
of acquisition—the things "everybody" has. As advertisers aim
at younger and younger audiences, the pressure reaches pre-
teens too.

Alex pursued several professional positions, none of which
had worked out. Though Alex was never completely unem-

ployed—"I always found things to do," he says—he often found himself working below his ability and credentials. As their son Matt came into his teenage years, he and Kristin found the financial pressures growing. Alex remembers:

We tried to protect him, which was pretty futile. Our financial worries were too obvious both physically and emotionally. Matt became very resentful and angry when it became obvious he was facing another move because of Dad not having a regular job. Our feelings fluctuated between giving Matt some noble ideal of living simply—and guilt over depriving our child.

Kristin adds:

I used to sit down with Matt and tell him, "Your friends have all of these things but we just don't have the money." He'd say, "Just write a check." And he'd say things like, "I'm going to have a Lamborghini and people working for me when I grow up." We would feel guilty because we had made him this way.

But Kristin and Alex also remember ways the Lord provided for them and helped them cope with Matt's needs:

Once Matt wanted a $160 tennis racket. We gave him $40, and he got a job as a paper boy to earn the rest of the money to buy it. We lived in a ritzy area of town where the kids all dressed preppy. In the summer I'd buy up all these clothes on sale. Matt was small and children's sizes would still fit him. The church provided scholarships for youth camp. The leader would call me and ask about our need privately.

Alex now has a steady job, and the family is getting their bills paid. Together Alex, Kristin and Matt are deciding how to use their money wisely. They haven't found a perfect formula or solution, but they're working on it together.

There's enjoyment in freely deciding to use our money wisely and imaginatively. In the process, we may decide we don't need things we thought we needed or that the world insists we need.

When Joel found himself unemployed following his wife's career move to a small town, at first he looked everywhere for work. Then he asked himself: "Do we need the second income, or is time more necessary for keeping things going in the household? Do I need to work, or is that society's expectation? Or my expectation?"

After a time Joel relaxed about his job search and got involved in many community activities. It did mean some changes in their lifestyle, which he admits they're still working through. Joel puts it in graphic form: We assume careers are a progression upward:

but usually they are more like this:

Of course Joel's unemployment situation is not acute because his wife has a well-paying career. But what if we're not in that situation? What do we do when the money is about to stop or has already stopped? What if the wolf is at the front door, and panic is knocking at the back door? How will we pay our bills?

Some people don't care if they pay their bills or not, but Christians have a responsibility to keep financial commitments and pay what we owe. If we don't, our word becomes meaningless. If we're unemployed and in debt, the worst thing we can do is to get further into debt. Yet many unemployed people do exactly that.

Being unemployed puts us short of cash to pay our bills. So it may seem to make sense to start charging more than ever, even to pay bills by credit card. "Many people feel a need to spend more when they are unemployed. The good feelings that come with a purchase are coupled with a belief that things purchased on credit really don't have to be paid back, at least not very soon."[1] Nothing could set us up for more discouragement and eventual disaster. As the New American Standard Bible puts it: "The borrower becomes the lender's slave" (Proverbs 22:7).

If that last line sounds too real, and you find yourself thinking about which bills you can put off each week, you may already have a problem. There are many helpful books, such as chapter ten of *Debt-Free Living* by Larry Burkett (Moody Press, 1989). There are also credit counseling services offered by family services, credit unions, and religious organizations. We have seen many favorable references to the Consumer Credit Counseling Services (CCCS). To find the location nearest you, call 1-800-388-2227. This is a nonprofit organization which offers help with budgeting and when necessary renegotiation of payments with creditors. Avoid credit repair clinics which offer the same service for large fees or consolidation loans as the only solution.

If your income has dried up, or is about to, the first thing to do is to stop charging things, and try, try, try to do all possible to keep paying off outstanding bills. Even a little at a time is better than letting them go. Most stores and services will work with us and carry us if they see us making the effort by regularly paying something. It's when they don't hear from us at all that they want to start legal action, and we get the reputation of deadbeats. (It is interesting to note that we use the term *deadbeats* here to mean "people who don't pay their bills." Credit card companies now use the term to mean "people who pay their balance every month and avoid finance charges." Whether we're employed or not, it pays to be a "deadbeat" in the second sense!)

Take Stock
More likely, your income hasn't dried up completely just be-

cause your job is gone. Add up every bit of continuing income you can still expect: for example, rental property, investment income, interest, money owed you by others who can be reasonably expected to pay. It's often the case that one spouse is still working. How much can you expect from his or her job? Do you still have another part-time job, no matter how small? Each source of income may not seem much, but it all helps.

Be sure to contact your unemployment compensation office to check your eligibility for unemployment benefits, how much you're eligible to receive, when you can start collecting and for how long. What severance pay and vacation benefits will you receive from your former employer? What is the total amount of cash available to you in checking and savings accounts?

What additional assets can be freed in the near future, such as certificates which will be maturing? How much is available to borrow from life insurance policies? Are there other assets you can sell?

You'll need to consider a substantial portion of these additional assets, along with any credit cards, as an emergency fund for unexpected expenses. The rest can be used to figure a monthly budget. To make a working budget, divide your expenses among several different categories:

Continuing (Fixed):
Taxes
Mortgage or rent
Loan payments
Tithe (if amount of income is predictable)

Continuing (Flexible):
Food
Telephone
Utilities
Tithe (if amount of income is unpredictable)

Occasional (But may be whoppers):
Insurance premiums
Medical costs
Tuition
Property taxes

Discretionary (Expenses which are not necessary or may be put off):
Clothing
Gifts
Entertainment
Recreation

For the most part there is little we can do to change our fixed expenses. If you realize you are not going to be able to pay them on time, try to arrange partial payment or an alternative payment plan in advance. If some of the loans are for things you don't need or use regularly (such as recreational vehicles), consider selling them and paying off the loan to cut expenses.

The second category, flexible, offers the most choices for how to make your money go further. Here we discover many choices about the quantity and quality of the products and services we have to pay for. Buying fewer prepared foods, writing notes instead of calling long-distance, and taking charge of the lights and thermostat—they all help us get a handle on flexible expenses. If you cringe at the idea of "cutting back"— and who doesn't?—chapter four will give some creative ideas for doing it successfully without feeling like a helpless victim of circumstances.

Occasional expenses don't offer much opportunity to save, but we have to take them into account in order to have the money available when they come due. If we don't have savings from which to draw, or if we hesitate to pay those occasional expenses out of savings, we have to start putting money aside in advance—in a separate account or at least in our own figuring. If money isn't available when those bills come due, we may find ourselves deciding between eating and paying the bill!

Listing all our expenses in order is not done to depress us. It's done to give us a clear picture of where our money has been going and must now go. It lets us choose in advance where to cut back in order to have cash available for things that matter to us. If we don't decide now, the decision will be made arbitrarily on an emergency basis, and we probably won't like the results.

Next, go back over the flexible and discretionary lists of expenses, and decide what is really important to you and your family. By all means involve the whole family in the decisions. It will take the whole family's cooperation to make the budget work. Better to have the give-and-take necessary during the planning stage than to put up with conflicts and blow-ups resulting from surprises later.

At this point you may ask, as Alex did, "How do you budget a non-income?" Maybe the money has already dried up. It just isn't there and doesn't look like it's going to be there. Hard as it is, this is the best time to remember that the Lord has not gone out of business. He still cares. Our experience and the experience of many is that he delights in providing for us in the least expected ways. Joyce remembers a particularly wrenching time when the Lord showed himself faithful to their family:

When our daughter was two years old I went to the store with just 25¢ to get a loaf of bread. With tax it came to 26¢. The checker said, "That will be 26¢."

I said, "I've only got a quarter, I guess I'll have to put it back." She said, "I guess you will."

Meanwhile there were other people waiting impatiently in line. I could just hear them thinking, "Just give her the penny and go on."

I put the bread back, but I was really feeling angry about it. I felt like just putting the bread under my coat and walking out. I finally put it back and went out to the car and cried.

About 6:00 that evening someone brought us a large bag of food. They said it was things that they would never use. To us they were normal everyday foods we could use.

Temporary Work

Miracles do happen, but we can also supplement our income in other ways besides the miraculous. Temporary or part-time work is often easier to find than permanent full-time employment. Either will provide income while you continue to look for more attractive and suitable work.

During our time in the Chicago area, a short-term ghost-writing/secretarial job came to an end for Sandy, and there was nothing to follow it up. A musician friend told us that he had been working for a temporary agency between the end of his teaching job and taking a new job. I had never even heard of temporary agencies, or if I had, I didn't remember.

I called the agency my friend worked for and arranged to take their secretarial test. I went to the agency's office exactly once, the day I took the test. After that, for three years, if there was a job—and there usually was—they would call me, and I would show up at the time and place they sent me. If I was tied up, say with a writing deadline, I could turn down the job with no problem.

I worked for anything and everything: a huge insurance company, a one-person collection agency, a philanthropic foundation, the test kitchens of a famous food company, a musical-instrument maker that was about to go under, and dozens of others. My bosses ranged from wonderful to scarcely human. Office spaces went from gorgeous to grungy. Office machines were everything from state-of-the-art to prehistoric.

The work itself was not very challenging, except that I had to learn new procedures and adjust to new personalities every time I walked into a different office. Usually they needed a temp because they had a work overload so the office was very busy. Sometimes, filling in for a vacationing secretary, I twiddled my thumbs. (What executive would admit he or she could get by for a week without a secretary?) I could cope with each job because I knew it was temporary.

A temp job can also lead to a permanent position. The best-kept secret about temp agencies is that businesses use them as employment agencies to try out potential workers. As Robert Half puts it, "What better way for an employer to judge someone than to watch that person at work every day for a week or two, or even longer? Hiring someone represents a great unknown to employers, no matter how diligent they've been in evaluating a résumé, asking probing questions during an interview, and checking references. A temporary worker who has been on the job quickly becomes a known entity."[2] If you can tolerate bouncing from workplace to workplace, temporary work gets your foot in the door at places you might not otherwise even get an interview.

Although I was not looking for one, I was offered several full-time jobs because employers knew exactly what they would get. A word of caution: if you accept a permanent job at a place where you've worked as a temp, you don't know exactly what you're going to get. True, you've seen the place from the inside, usually at its worst under the stress of a work overload. But working there for two weeks is not the same as working there forever. One office did persuade me to leave the temp agency to take a part-time job with them. When they gave us antique variable-space typewriters without lift-off ribbons—and outlawed the use of Korectype or Liquid Paper because they had off-white stationery—I went back to the temp agency!

What About McDonalds?
Every unemployed person we talked with, and probably every unemployed person you've met, said, "I could always go work

at McDonalds" (or Burger King, or Hardees, or whatever). They say it, but few actually go and do it, preferring to remain unemployed instead. Is it a good strategy to resist taking a low-pay, low-status job while waiting for the real thing to come along?

Norm never actually did it, but he reflects on what such a job could mean for a Christian:

> Sure it's humbling to go to work at a fast-food place when you're used to something more. But it may not be out of God's will to take something lower to work pride out of us. I remember seeing a former pastor working at Hardees for a while. The guy just had a glow. You could see Jesus in his face. It wouldn't be a permanent position for him, but for right then it made him a blessing.

In *The Complete Job-Search Handbook,* Howard Figler praises the value of working at jobs outside or "beneath" your usual career while you're searching for what you really want:

> The interim job is not the one you want, but it may be the one you need right now. . . . The interim job gives you some breathing room, some room to maneuver and rest your big guns until the target job is available and you're ready for it. . . . You can work to improve the skills you need to go after the target job. . . . If your recent work record had something go wrong, the interim job can give you a positive work experience to call on, a good reference to use for the next position. . . . It can even give you time for personal projects that you have been wanting to do, since the interim job may require less intense involvement than a target job.[3]

No doubt there are many part-time job opportunities in your area which can provide some income and the time flexibility you need to carry on your active job search. The pay may not be high, but it will give you more time to research career opportunities and find the job you really want. Also, as Figler points out, "Many fine careers have begun with part-time employment, where you and the boss have a chance to get to know each other without any great pressure."[4]

Consider the story of a young woman who took a job as a hotel desk clerk after searching unsuccessfully for a position as an assistant manager:

> The pay was awful, the clientele overbearing, and the sight of her friends registering at the hotel was almost more than she could stand. But a manager noticed her efforts on behalf of important guests, and she became first in line for the management training program. During the interim, Ann had also taken computer skills courses and public speaking courses to sharpen her qualifications for the opportunity she knew would develop eventually. Without the interim job she would have been a less qualified candidate.[5]

A Little Help from My Friends

Phil found his Christian friends to be a tremendous resource when he was suddenly unemployed. "Other Christians who knew of things to be done would tell me about work. That's how the body of Christ functioned. Also I've been trades-oriented all my life so I knew people and had contacts for doing painting, construction and so forth."

All of us have skills which somebody—maybe a lot of people—can occasionally use. Working as a handyman, painter, piano teacher, typist, lawn mower, tutor, consultant, or whatever you have to offer is another way to add income while maintaining flexibility for a job search. Letting a few friends know you are available will sometimes get you started. A small ad in the paper is often effective.

When we came back from two years overseas, we weren't sure where we were going to live or what we were going to do. A widow asked Dale to spade up her garden. She told someone else about him, and over time he landed numerous other jobs as a general handyman. Over the years we have often depended on Dale's handyman skills to provide additional income (and for some periods of time our only income).

In a Revised Standard Version Bible we were using at that time, Psalm 31:15 is circled: "My times are in thy hand." Next to it is the date 11/30/73. That was precisely the time we were wondering what to do next. God was faithful then and has continued to be faithful leading us through the various "times," including times of unemployment and irregular employment.

This chapter has presented some options for "buying time" when we're out of work. You'll probably think of many more. But however you buy time, remember that the Lord is the Lord of time. He will provide all the time you need to do what you have to do to make it.

The days of the blameless are known to the Lord,
and their inheritance will endure forever.
In times of disaster they will not wither;
in days of famine they will enjoy plenty.
(Psalm 37:19)

Things to Do

☐ Continue to be generous in your giving, knowing that God will supply all of your needs.

☐ Make a budget to help find ways to make your income go further.

☐ Look for temporary or part-time work to give you more time to find permanent work.

☐ Remember all of your time is ultimately in God's hands.

Suggested Reading

Burkett, Larry. *Debt-Free Living.* Chicago, Ill.: Moody Press, 1989. The problem of both national and private debt in the U.S. at large is discussed. See especially the chapters on budgeting and the reasons why people go into debt.

Cohen, Charles E. "The Last Charge." *Ladies' Home Journal,* June 1991, pp. 118-25. The story of a family of four who were

doing great—till Dad's wages were cut by $34,000. How they
started digging themselves out of debt.

Half, Robert. *How to Get a Better Job in This Crazy World.* New
York, N.Y.: Crown Publishers, 1990. The author says, "If I
had to boil down this book to one suggestion for getting a
better job in this crazy world, it would be get smart. And don't
stop learning until you stop breathing." Readable, up-to-date
and often humorous help.

Irish, Richard K. *Go Hire Yourself an Employer.* Revised and ex-
panded ed. New York, N.Y.: Anchor Press/Doubleday, 1987.
An informally written nuts-and-bolts book about finding
what Irish calls a "judgment job"—a job you do because you
want to do it, which allows the exercise of talent and ad-
dresses real needs in the world at large.

Krannich, Ronald L. and Caryl Rae. *Network Your Way to Job &*
Career Success. Manassas, Va.: Impact Publications, 1989.
Good advice on drawing on other people without "using"
people. Emphasizes honesty in the job-hunting process.

Perry, Richard D. *Money Problems.* Elgin, Ill.: David C. Cook
Publishing Co., 1987. Looks at "the spiritual and emotional
reasons people have problems with money" and practical
ways out of a financial jam. Though written as part of the
"Helping Others in Crisis" series, it has plenty of practical
advice we can all apply to ourselves.

4

Doing More on Less or Living High on the Hog on a Pig-Hock Budget

We all know the Lord will provide for us,
but a lot depends on your personality.
Some people just naturally expect the worst.
Others expect the best.
Robert, former teacher

Give me neither poverty nor riches,
but give me only my daily bread.
Otherwise, I may have too much and disown you
and say, "Who is the LORD?"
Or I may become poor and steal,
and so dishonor the name of my God.
Proverbs 30:8-9

Reader's guarantee: This chapter is almost sure to save you the price of this book!

Last April during one of our frequent times of unemployment, we went down to visit Sandy's mother in southern Illinois, then stopped by the Chicago area to see editors at several of our publishers. It had been too cold to camp around where we live in northern Wisconsin, so we planned to take advantage of the trip "south" to go camping near the historic town of Galena, Illinois.

At a bookstore in the Chicago suburbs we discovered a whole room full of drastically marked-down new books. They had to kick us out at 9:00 p.m. when the store closed. (They would have done better to just lock us in and let us check out our purchases the next morning.) One of our "finds" was a book on free campsites all over the U.S.—including one near Galena, Illinois, where we were headed the next day. The book cost $4.00.

We camped two nights at the free campground, which turned out to be at a boat landing on the Mississippi River. It's free because it isn't officially open till Memorial Day; you can camp there, but the water and electricity aren't turned on yet. That was fine since we're used to primitive camping.

Boat landings (sad to say) are terrific places to pick up aluminum cans to turn in for cash. The price was down, but we picked up a big bagful anyway because we believe in recycling and since it certainly helped the looks of the place. When we got back home, a local scrap-iron place was offering a one-day special price for aluminum far above the going rate. That day there was a line-up of pickup trucks full of cans. Our single bag came to something like $3.87. Too busy to make change, the man said "Here, close enough," and handed over $4.00. Which, of course, precisely paid for the book on free campsites. Total cost of camping: $0, plus we still own the book.

Living on Less
There are people who will think our story is great, and there are people who will be appalled at the thought of scrounging cans for pennies and camping without electricity or running water. If you're the second kind of person, the crisis of unemployment will not instantly make you into the first kind of person. Just because your income has dried up and you know you have to spend less, that doesn't mean you automatically like the idea. The thought of cutting back may be excruciating. You feel you can't. You know you've got to. But how?

There are plenty of books out on how to live on next to nothing. The problem is, if we're used to living comfortably, that's the last thing we want to read. Besides, some of it has a self-righteous ring. What we want to know is not how to exist on corn husks and unflavored gelatin, but how to live well—which is to say, enjoyably—on a suddenly shrunken budget.

It seems an impossible dream. But you can do it. You can enjoy life on shockingly less money than you think. We aren't necessarily talking about living in a cabin and having two changes of clothes and eating pinto beans every night, although that's great if you find it acceptable and satisfying. We're talking about having comforts, having fun, having pleasant surroundings, having good food, having entertainment, while spending far less than most people think possible.

It takes creativity . . . art . . . imagination . . . a spirit of adventure. It often takes time, but that's something you have more of now. It also takes a renewed faith in a good and loving God.

Do you ever get the impression that God doesn't want us to enjoy life? That he wants us to avoid material comforts at all cost? It's true, Jesus warned against the dangers of materialism with words such as, "Do not store up for yourselves treasures on earth, where moth and rust destroy, and thieves break in and steal" (Matthew 6:19), and "The one who received the seed that fell among the thorns is the man who hears the word, but the worries of this life and the deceitfulness of wealth choke it, making it unfruitful" (Matthew 13:22). However, what Jesus called dangerous was not the material things themselves, but the love of them and the craving for them. He called us to trust God to provide all we need. "And why do you worry about clothes? See how the lilies of the field grow. They do not labor or spin. Yet I tell you that not even Solomon in all his splendor was dressed like one of these" (Matthew 6:28-29).

Enjoy What You Have

Our problem is that the craving for "more" keeps us from enjoying the good things that are already ours. As long as we stay in a mad pursuit of more things, we find little time or reason to enjoy the things God has already given us. And we certainly aren't thankful for what he has provided if we insist it's not enough.

Look around. Why not break out those "good" items you've got safely stored away in the basement or the spare bedroom? For example, the wedding presents that are too special to use for every day (or any day), or the party clothes (worn once for a special occasion) that you don't have anyplace to wear. Enjoy them. They're paid for, aren't they?

The reasons for staging this Christmas in July or unbirthday party are more psychological than physical. It's nice to use the stuff, but even more than that, it's a way to treat yourself to something special that doesn't cost you anything. It says you're a valuable person. If you don't like or need some of the stuff you unearth, have a high-class garage sale and get a little extra cash!

Okay, you've plundered the back closet and you've rediscovered treasures you forgot you owned. It's been a mini-windfall. But there are basic necessities of life beyond silver salad tongs and gas barbecue grills. There are things you're going to have to purchase, and it seems the money to do it just won't be there.

For a long time we have personally lived with the dilemma of having expensive taste on an income which occasionally plays tag with the national poverty line and never stays very far ahead. We have discovered that "better a meal of vegetables where there is love than a fattened calf with hatred" (Proverbs 15:17). We have also discovered that we can eat the vegetables off gold-rimmed plates, and, every now and then, we can even have the fattened calf.

In spite of extreme budget limitations, every night we sit

down to candlelight dinners with crystal goblets and English bone china. The food usually measures up to the setting in appearance and flavor. (While working on this chapter, Sandy got to reading a new magazine and burned a beautiful Oriental dinner to a crisp, but that's unusual.) We are able to dine this way because we have chosen to restrict ourselves in other areas—not out of self-denial, but in order to free enough money to have some things we really enjoy.

China and crystal may leave you cold. All right. The point is, think of the areas of life where it's important to you to have some elegance, and identify the ones you don't care all that much about. Then choose the direction in which the most of your limited money will go.

Choose Well

Maybe you feel you have no choice. The money has to go for food, clothing, housing and transportation. That's true. But what kind of food, clothing, housing and transportation will you choose to purchase for your limited amount of cash?

Some would say you have to choose the cheapest. (Otherwise known as the cruddiest, shabbiest and most embarrassing.)

Not necessarily. According to Proverbs, appearances don't tell the entire tale: "One man pretends to be rich, yet has nothing; another pretends to be poor, yet has great wealth" (Proverbs 13:7).

We happen to love prowling through resale shops and discount places (like our orgy in the bookstore above). If you haven't shopped in such places, you won't believe the gems you can unearth there—if you look for them. Some items at resale shops are new, with the tags still on them. Some of the cheapest discount stores have buyers with wonderful taste.

We have discovered that among friends who love this kind of buying, a certain one-upmanship can even develop. ("You got this one-of-a-kind hand-carved walnut table and six chairs for $150? Well, we got our six-foot antique buffet free because somebody was throwing it away.") Maybe that kind of talk turns you off. Okay, you don't have to tell anybody where you found your elegant, long, wool-tweed-"Sherlock-Holmes" topcoat (at the used-clothing store) or how much you paid for it ($10). (By the way, all the examples above are real.)

What about everybody's most pressing daily expense: food? If you're a married man, you may be thinking, "Look, my wife does all the cooking, and she's the one who still has a job!" If that's your case, you fit the current pattern of unemployment in America. Well, some of the best chefs in the world are men. There's no reason you can't learn to do some of it yourself. You will find good basic cookbooks at the public library.

Spending less for food doesn't have to mean living on soup bones and beans. It's surprising how much we can save by buying basic foods and spending a little more time in the kitchen preparing them, rather than buying prepackaged dinners, instant foods, and salty corn snacks.

As for the packaged snack foods, they can be replaced with popcorn, and it's healthier. If the flavor bores you, try seasoned salt or other seasonings for variety. Breakfast cereals mixed with some peanuts and raisins and toasted with butter and seasonings also make tasty snacks.

"Butter?" you wonder. "Aren't we talking about cutting back?"

The point is, you choose what to splurge on and what to skimp on. If you don't want to give up the taste of real butter, then cut back on something else.

And yes, Virginia, there is such a thing as free food. There's a stigma about accepting USDA food handouts, but if your income is low enough that you qualify for them (things like peanut butter, dry milk, canned goods, and cheese) by all means don't be too proud to go get them. These surplus food products are bought up by the federal government to support farm prices (thus staving off unemployment for farmers!). Their quality is excellent because you get them earlier in the food-processing chain, before they are diluted, stretched, whipped and fluffed by food manufacturers. (We don't have that word officially from the USDA, but it's something we've observed.)

Now a word about name-brand products—not only food, but all kinds of things. No doubt a few of them are really worth the extra price, but for many items the difference between a store brand and the higher-priced name brand is not noticeable. Check product ratings in *Consumer Reports*. It's amusing how often an obscure store brand is rated above a famous brand. With certain items, such as liquid bleach and aspirin, the active ingredients are identical.

If you can't stand the idea of seeing "generic" products around the house, there are even some tricks for that. Much of the high-quality feel of name brands comes not from the products themselves but from their pizzazzy packaging. Buy one particularly attractive package of something high-priced, then when it's used up, buy the generic and put it into the luxury package. The quality of the generic is usually close to the name brand, and often better, and you still get to handle the familiar package and feel like you're using the luxury item. (Obviously products like shampoo and dishwashing liquid are better candidates than toothpaste and pop-up tissues.) If you think that's a dumb idea, then forget it—but don't forget it till you've tried it once.

Change Your Surroundings

The aim of all these gimmicks is as much psychological as financial. Perhaps your biggest psychological influence is your living space, especially since you're spending more time there than you used to. Suddenly, you notice everything that's wrong with your house. This wall is starting to crack and that floor is badly scratched, and you never noticed how the deck is sagging downward and outward. Where are you going to get the money to fix all this?

Several years ago we were going through a very discouraging period of underemployment. We were looking for more meaningful work and anticipated that we would move soon. We were renting a little gem of a cottage and were very happy with it, but it had some problems that nagged at us. The interior had obviously been painted in a hurry just before we moved in. The white paint was peeling off the gray furnace tape which had been used to patch the cracks in the walls. Thick layers of old wallpaper under the paint were bulging where they had pulled away from the walls of our bedroom. Our landlord had said we could redecorate, but we held off, thinking, "We'll be moving soon anyway."

"Soon" turned into weeks, then months. Finally, we decided that even though we didn't know how much longer we would stay in that place, we could at least make it more enjoyable while we were there.

The next week wasn't that much more enjoyable, unless you enjoy being surrounded with masses of soggy old wallpaper. But the new coat of wedgewood blue paint really brightened the bedroom and went very well with the cross-stitch quilt Sandy had made. It also brightened our spirits for the next year or so that we lived there.

Most home-improvement projects take more time than money, assuming you do the work yourself. You'll gain in several ways. You'll make your living space more pleasant, which boosts your sense of well-being. You'll successfully complete a task which gives you a tangible reward—something you deeply need since your job no longer gives you that. You'll have a sense of accomplishment and mastery. And you'll add to the value of your home and make it more salable should your new job take you to a new location.

Do you break out in a cold sweat at the thought of tackling a home repair job? Do you only envision (or does your spouse envision) how you'll make it worse and have to call in a professional to redo what you did? Well, if you've followed this book so far, you pass the first qualification: you can read directions. You'll find instructions for doing almost anything in books at the public library. Look for the most basic book, and don't be ashamed to ask for help from knowledgeable people; they're usually glad to show off their knowledge.

There's a balance here. We need to stretch our abilities without setting ourselves up for failure. If you've hardly driven a nail in your life, this is not the time to take on building a new garage (or even tearing down your old one by yourself). Start with something simple while you develop your skills. For example, if this is the first time you have ever tried painting, don't start with a front door full of little windows. A wall in a spare room is much less demanding, and besides, why advertise your amateur status on the front door for all to see?

Fifteen years ago Dale reupholstered an Art Nouveau loveseat in exactly this manner (getting a book at the library and following the directions). It's starting to fade, and the next time I do it I will no doubt add some fancy tucks and buttons to the back. At the time, for my first upholstering project, I stuck to a straightforward design.

Stenciling is a ridiculously easy project which adds luxury details to any room. The stencils can be made from old file folders. Substitute sponges or cheap foam paintbrushes for expensive stencil brushes. It takes so little paint that you can use what's left in the bottom of the can from some other project. Warning: Stenciling is so easy that once you get the stencil in one hand and the paint-daubed sponge in the other hand, you'll stencil everything in sight. Restrain yourself to good taste.

With a little practice you will find you can do far more than you thought you could. The feeling of accomplishment is sure to brighten your mood. Just don't expect too much of yourself to begin with. It may take a little time to learn some of the skills you need.

Don't Become a Hermit

Now what about entertaining?

People going through unemployment typically withdraw socially right when we most need the support of other people. The reasons are not only financial. We don't want to hear that dreaded question "Have you found a job yet?" It's good to have ready a response that honestly answers the question but gives you the chance to change the subject. Something like, "Not yet, but I'm working on it. How are things with you?" Or use the question as an opportunity to do some "fishing": "No, have you heard of anything?"

If you have always enjoyed entertaining, don't give it up just because you have less money to spend. Invite some people for a potluck dinner. They'll invariably leave you with more food than you started with. If you think the idea of a potluck meal would turn your friends off, then specify it as a taco or sandwich party and ask people to bring their favorite taco ingredient or sandwich filler. You could even give a prize for the most creative sandwich. If people you know aren't used to bringing their own meat to a backyard cookout, then invite them to join you at a favorite park or beach. Everyone will bring their own food, then share with each other.

Can you entertain with all those unfinished projects around the house? Of course. Just say, "Excuse the mess, I'm redoing the kitchen" or "Pardon the smell of varnish, I'm refinishing this cherry writing desk." People will be terribly impressed and, probably, jealous of you for having the time to do that sort of thing.

Enjoy Hobbies

This time of unemployment can also be a good time to expand your areas of recreation. Dropping your membership in the local health club doesn't mean you start sitting at home doing nothing. Break out the bicycles and put them to use. A hike in the woods (or fields, or park, or whatever is handy) can be refreshing as well as healthy exercise, and free. Go to the library first and check out a field guide for birds, trees or wildflowers to add extra interest to your walk. It's a way to improve your knowledge and appreciation of God's creation as well as a great family activity you can all do together.

In any community there are all kinds of events a family can attend for free or very inexpensively. The quality may not be world-class, but you'll see something terrific: amateurs giving their all at what they love to do. Local softball leagues, gymnastics tournaments, art festivals, community theater, outdoor band concerts, fairs and carnivals, school plays and concerts—watch the newspaper or posters and see what's happening in your town. Or get involved yourself and let other people come and watch you!

You probably already rent movies to watch at home, but did you know you can get those at the library too? Recently we discovered another free source of home entertainment from the library: audio tapes, records and compact discs. This week we've been enjoying Vladimir Horowitz playing Beethoven sonatas, courtesy of our library.

And, please, don't forget reading. So much of American home entertainment is passive (watching something) that books get overlooked as a source of mind-expanding pleasure at home.

Take a Vacation

We can see that there are a lot of options for low-cost fun close to home. Sometimes, though, you and your family just need to get away from it all. How can you take a vacation when you don't have much money and you're determined not to exercise your credit cards?

One possibility: go camping.

We don't mean the version of "camping" where you purchase a luxury motor home, equip it with duplicates of everything in your house, and head off for a cross-country trip towing your car behind you. That's fine if you already own all that stuff, but unreasonable to buy while in an unemployed state. Besides, there are usually places much closer to home where you can spend just a couple of days for a pleasant break. Once school is out, you don't have to wait till the weekend, so you can even avoid the crowds.

The least expensive way to camp is tent-camping, and you'll do fine without the latest state-of-the-art model tent. You can buy all kinds of specialized camping gear, but you don't really need most of it. For example, unless you're going backpacking, special lightweight cooking pans are not necessary. Take your ordinary stuff from the kitchen (though if you cook over a wood fire, you'll probably want to pick up some extreme cheapies, since they'll turn black). Don't take anything you can't live without back home, since things do disappear in the grass or get left behind under picnic tables.

The tent, sleeping bags and camp stove will be your major investments, but they are long-life items you'll enjoy for years. Used ones turn up if you watch the ads in the paper. If you're hesitant to invest in any equipment at all because you're not sure camping is for you, you can often borrow equipment from a friend or rent it for a few days.

There will be mosquitoes and flies, and you'll find there were things you wish you'd brought and other things you don't know why you brought, and it may rain, but go with the flow. Camping can be terrific low-cost family fun.

In northern Michigan we camped next to a young couple who used camping to cope with periodic unemployment. They lived in southeastern Michigan, where the auto industry makes workers subject to layoffs. The husband would be out of work for weeks at a time. The kids weren't in school yet, so the whole family would head to the Upper Peninsula and camp out for

$4.00 or $5.00 a night. Every so often he would drive back home to cut the grass and check on the house. They had developed a pattern of living with slack times and making the best of them.

The pattern worked for that family because there was some assurance that the husband's job would still be there at the end of the layoff period. He wasn't actively out looking for a new job. But camping trips can be valuable for job exploration as well.

If you're wondering if the job market is better somewhere else, why guess? Go there if possible and combine the job-exploration trip with a family camping trip. Many campgrounds have showers, laundry facilities, and a place to plug in a blow-dryer and an iron. From your campsite vantage point you can make some "cold calls" and also check out the cost of living and the quality of life there.

In this chapter we've only shared some ideas from our own experience. We can't tailor-make these hints for your situation, nor do we have to. Take off from these ideas and invent your own. You'll be able to think of many we haven't thought of!

No matter how you decide how to stretch your limited re-sources, you don't have to put the pleasures of life on hold. You only need to use your imagination and your extra time to use your resources more creatively to discover new sources of pleas-ure.

Things to Do
☐ Treat yourself to the things you've been saving for a special occasion.

☐ Cut food costs with meals which use less prepared foods and low-cost snacks to replace more expensive ones.

☐ Do a labor-intensive home repair project which will increase the value of your home and give you a sense of accomplish-ment.

☐ Take a low-cost break with a short camping trip or day trip.

Suggested Reading

Davidson, Christine. *Staying Home Instead: How to Quit the Working-Mom Rat Race and Survive Financially.* Lexington, Mass.: D.C. Heath & Co., 1986. Though Christine Davidson is jobless by choice, rather than because of losing her job, her upbeat suggestions are good for any family getting by on less income.

Hatton, Hap, and Laura Torbet. *Helpful Hints for Hard Times: How to Live It Up While Cutting Down.* New York, N.Y.: Facts on File Publications, 1983. The title says it all.

Peel, Kathy. "Don't Buy It—Swap for It!" *Family Circle,* April 21, 1992, pp. 38-40. Ideas for "swap-it economics," flea-market negotiating and other creative dollar-stretchers.

Seixas, Suzanne. "Laid Off." *Money,* February 1991, pp. 78-86. How a 41-year-old middle manager and his family cope with his abrupt layoff. Includes advice to the family from a career consultant and a financial planner.

5

What Do You Really Want?

I thank God for the day I got fired.
It was the best thing that ever happened to me.
Blair, five years after being fired

A man can do nothing better than to eat and drink
and find satisfaction in his work.
This too, I see, is from the hand of God,
for without him, who can eat or find enjoyment?
Ecclesiastes 2:24-25

D o you think you could ever make a statement like Blair's above? Neither did Blair—not on the day he lost his job selling furniture in a retail store.

"At the time, it was the worst thing that ever happened to me," he admits. "It's only now, five years later, that I can say it was the best thing."

How could that be?

"Because it forced me to look at my abilities and realize I wasn't fully using them in the job I'd been doing."

Now Blair is building a new career as an interior decorator. He's using some of the same skills he used in the furniture store—putting people and home-decorating materials together—but now he gets to exercise his latent creativity.

Blair is able to look back and bless his job loss because he used it to take a closer look at his dreams and give them an opportunity to come back to life. When we've lost a job, our buried dreams are a good place to start looking to the future.

Dream Again

But isn't now an odd time to indulge in dreams? Haven't our dreams just been crushed? Besides, we have immediate needs— food on the table, a roof over our heads. Isn't this a time to be practical instead of reviving the past?

Yes, it's a time to be practical. It is very practical to take a fresh look at old dreams that got lost in the shuffle of surviving the daily grind. Those old dreams may hold the key to a happily employed future.

"What do you want to be when you grow up?" Every kid is put on the spot by grown-ups with that question. How did you answer it? When did your answers begin to change? The trauma of being out of work can jolt some lost aspirations back into the realm of possibility.

John Crystal and Richard Bolles have spent decades helping people find the careers they really want. In the early 1970s they wrote about dreams and job-hunting:

> Most people fail to find what they want in life for a very simple reason: they have cut down their original dream to one-eighth of its original size and strength; hence they are only hunting for one-eighth of their original dream—with only one-eighth of their heart (or gut). If you can recover *your whole dream*—what you really want to do with your life more than anything else, you will inevitably begin to *hunt for that whole vision with all of your heart (or gut)*. And how much you want something *does* affect whether or not you find it.[1]
> (Emphasis added.)

Remember Norm, the house painter from chapter two whose church helped him find release from bitterness after he lost his job? He says, about himself: "I'm the best example I know of a jack of all trades and master of none. At one time I wanted to be a missionary who could go to some remote place and stay there a couple of years doing anything and everything—whatever needed to be done." Now he says, "I don't know exactly what I want to do. All I know is that I'm not completely satisfied doing what I'm doing." Although he has learned to cope well emotionally and financially with his uncertain self-employment, Norm still feels dissatisfied. He confesses:

> I have a lot of ambitions and goals and I've done a lot of market analysis and research about what would fly in this area. For example, I'd like to have an auto-repair shop where we'd work on cars for people who can't afford regular shops. It would be job training for Christian young people, we'd have contemporary Christian music playing all the time and it would be a place for fellowship. The problem is, it all costs a lot of money.

Many of us have had our youthful dreams tarnished by cynicism or knocked down by economic realities. Those dreams deserve to be unpacked, polished and reappraised, and unemployment is the ideal time to do it. When we were working, we had neither time nor motivation to look at our former aspirations. Now we have more time and a compelling motivation. If we don't give our dreams another chance, we may grab whatever job comes along and then wonder why we still feel dissatisfied.

Freedom at Work

Interviews with younger men and women entering into the world of work reveal an interesting pattern: As they climb the organizational ladder, they often become less happy with their lives. What they thought they wanted isn't what they wanted at all. *What they thought they wanted was success when what they really wanted was to feel free.*[2] (Emphasis added.)

Does anybody really feel free at work? We can, if our work flows naturally from the passions and gifts God has put within us.

While we were working on this book, we had some computer glitches. Certain chapters wouldn't load—that is, they were on the disk, but the program wouldn't let us read them. Then, as outside temperatures plummeted, our office heater kept going out. Our phone went dead. An important article for this chapter was lost—misfiled or maybe even thrown out. Deadlines loomed. Still we never felt that frantic, exhausted, overloaded burnout—that sense of pointless despair—that comes in other jobs when things go wrong.

Why the difference? Because our work is feeding us instead of draining us. It refreshes our souls instead of eating away at our souls.

Janis Long Harris says this happy kind of work happens when we are using our "gifted passion":

When your gifts and your passions converge, you have a gifted passion—a passion supported by your gifts. . . . If you have a gifted passion and are able to incorporate it into your vocation you have a very good chance of loving your work. But if your vocation is based on gifts alone, without passion, or passions that are not supported by gifts, it's unlikely that you'll be able to love your work—at least not for very long.[3]

Nick was a gifted musician who had been attending church from the time he was six weeks old. He went to a Christian college and then to a Bible school, studying piano and organ the whole time. "I became a church musician because everybody told me I should become a church musician," he says now. "They took it for granted the only place for my talents was in the church, and I listened to them."

In a series of jobs as church music director, Nick's artistic vision clashed with conservative Christian style.

Eventually, he felt he had to choose, and he rejected biblical Christianity for a New Age blend. Now he sits and plays jazz alone as his communication with God—recognizing it's not the God of the Bible.

Sadly, Nick is still working as a church music director. "It's just a job," he says. "I show up, I do my job, I leave." Nick still has his God-given gifts, but his passion for church music is gone.

When our work comes from a gifted passion, we will work without coercion or role-playing, and we will find joy in our work.

What Is Your Passion?

Now is the time for brainstorming. Start writing down every dream, accomplishment, and hope you have had for your life. Make a list of everything you enjoy doing and the things that give you a sense of satisfaction. Don't leave anything out just because it sounds stupid or is unrealistic. Don't skip something because it represents the disappointment of a broken dream that at one time didn't work.

Remember those obscure magazines Sandy got to read on temp jobs? One had a list of "99 Idea Killers"—things we say that burst each other's creative balloons. Here are some of the choicest "idea killers" (since Sandy did the choosing, that probably means "the ones she's been told most often"):

"It's not our image."

"It's not our style."

"It'll cost a fortune!"

"We've never done anything like that."

"Let's meet on that some day."

"They won't let you."

"Let's be realistic."

"People will say we're silly."

"People will say we're reckless."

"What will people say?"

And Sandy's two favorites:

(Laughter)

and

(Silence)[4]

We need to be careful of saying such things to each other, but we also need to be careful of saying them to ourselves. As it says at the bottom of the list, "No idea is born perfect. Give it a chance to grow." That includes our own ideas about what we'd like to do.

Into what kind of work will our gifted passions lead us? Certainly it will be work which meets human needs.

The following notice recently appeared in our local paper: "Services were scheduled Sunday and Monday for Allan W. Adams, who with his father and brother were pioneers in the snack food industry. Adams died Thursday of cancer at age 81. . . . Adams was listed in *Who's Who in the World, Who's Who in the Midwest,* and *Who's Who in Finance and Industry.*"[5] What did Allan W. Adams of Beloit, Wisconsin, do to earn himself such eulogizing? He invented Korn Kurls. America did not even know it needed Korn Kurls until Allan W. Adams founded the Adams Corporation to manufacture them. The company was sold to Beatrice Foods in 1961, and the rest is history inscribed on orange-stained pages.

From a Christian view, the world has needs that won't be met with corny puffs of air. So many needs are left unmet because they get overlooked in the drive for profit-making. They stay unmet until (like a sacred version of Allan W. Adams) someone dreams of doing something about them—and does it.

Did you ever dream about making this a better world, perhaps bringing hope to the hopeless or the gospel to the lost? Did you ever dedicate your life to Christian service, perhaps at camp or a youth meeting? Our long-buried dreams and hidden goals may be God's voice leading us back to those ideals and into places of service where we can meet needs no one else is meeting.

Maybe you don't think you ever had such ideals. But do you have heroes? Our heroes tell us about ourselves, says Richard K. Irish—at least about the people we long to be.

Everybody is a hero worshiper. And staking out people we would like to be says to our secret selves that we could be like them. Reading the biographies of celebrated achievers in any walk of life puts you in the shoes of men and women, usually long dead, who continue to mold the future through the dreams of people like yourself.[6]

Who are your heroes (male and female)? If you have none today, who were your childhood heroes? If your hero was the Lone Ranger, don't feel silly. What was it about the masked man that you admired? The way he combined decency with an action-packed life? The way he did good deeds while remaining anonymous? His cross-cultural friendship with Tonto?

Irish suggests another practical activity for identifying our dreams: "keeping a file of advertisements, want ads, and news stories." He continues, "Unconsciously your psyche is self-selecting what interests you. Tearing out and filing every item you find yourself reading identifies products, services, problems, and target populations suggesting certain lines of work."[7]

Assess Yourself

The next question is, How much of our dream can we do? Remember, in order to be a "gifted passion," a dream must be accompanied by ability.

In *The New Quick Job-Hunting Map,* Richard Bolles suggests what he calls a "memory net." It is basically a chart showing dates, jobs and places as a reference to help you list your best activities and accomplishments. Another helpful book is Henry G. Pearson's *Your Hidden Skills: Clues to Careers and Future Pursuits,* in which you identify "transkills" which can be applied to a future job. It's important not to confine these skills too narrowly:

Most skills valued in work have the virtue of cutting a wide swatch across many occupational boundaries. For example, the ability to write effectively and in clear language is valued highly in private industry, government agencies, educational institutions, and nonprofit organizations alike. In fact, most of the skills that are important in any responsible job have a similar virtue: they can be applied in a wide variety of work contexts to a wide variety of tasks. They are transferable.[8] There are many self-assessment tests and techniques by which you can take stock of what you can do. They range from simple exercises to book-length courses. They are fun and can reveal surprising areas of strength for which you never gave yourself credit. However, Ronald Krannich cautions that most of these exercises do not encourage you to break out of past patterns of behavior and interest.[9]

In other words, if you've worked as an auto mechanic for fifteen years and have decided you want to teach college English instead, your skills/experience tests will still be overloaded on the manual and mechanical end—an accurate picture of what you can do but not very affirming of what you'd like to do. And at this point you want to untie yourself from previous set roles and give God freedom to lead you in unexpected directions.

Know Your Spiritual Gifts

Our local schools have a "gifted and talented" program for certain students. But in truth everyone is gifted and talented in some way (or ways). Christians have the further certainty that we are gifted by the Holy Spirit with certain abilities for the good of others. First Corinthians says: "There are different kinds of gifts, but the same Spirit. There are different kinds of service, but the same Lord. There are different kinds of working, but the same God works all of them in all men. Now to each one the manifestation of the Spirit is given for the common good" (1 Corinthians 12:4-7).

Ephesians 4 and 1 Corinthians 12 are the Scripture passages usually cited to identify the gifts of God's Spirit, though spiritual gifts are sprinkled throughout the Scripture. Our spiritual gifts are not always expressed through our work, but they may be.

There are many Bible studies about finding our spiritual gifts. Most include tests and questionnaires to determine your own gifts. They can be helpful, though like the skills tests in job-hunting books, they tend to test our experience rather than our joys—that is, what we have done rather than what we'd like to do.

Realistic Dreaming

In the midst of all this dreaming, we must face some realities of being limited creatures in a limited world. There may be reasons why our specific dreams can never become a literal reality. For example, a 40-year-old woman watches the female Olympic gymnasts and remembers her childhood sensation of near-flight on a backyard trampoline. It's too late for her to go back and become an Olympic gymnast, but her dreams give real clues to where her heart is.

For other people, like Virgil Marinelli of Lima, Ohio, it may not take a very large adjustment to make a dream come true. For twenty years Marinelli played Santa to sick and needy children. Every Christmas he spent an average of $3,000 on presents, sometimes raising money from friends, usually paying most of it himself. As his wife, Judy, puts it, "This guy puts on his Santa suit, and he can't say no."

But one year Santa Claus had no money. When his own family had staggering medical expenses, "Santa" Marinelli went bankrupt. Struggling to pay off his debts, his savings gone, he was still determined to play Santa.

"Here it was, Saturday morning, and Christmas was on Monday," Virgil recalls. "The welfare department phones and says, 'We forgot 80 kids, and we're out of money. Can you help?' I told Judy, 'That's it, give me the checkbook— whatever's in there is gone.' We went to Dollar General Store and bought everything left in the $4 to $7 price range. We spent $500 in all."

Judy adds, "We started going to the houses not knowing if the kids would be boys or girls, and at one there was the sweetest little girl. Virgil dug into his bag without even looking and pulled out a doll. I thought, 'Virgil, somebody above is watching over you.' "[10]

Money magazine doesn't usually celebrate the blessings of poverty, but Marinelli's story so touched the editor that he wrote: "The rich are the people who know you can't measure true wealth in dollars."[11]

Virgil "Santa" Marinelli knows what he wants to do. He can't afford to do it, but he is doing it anyway. In the meantime he is also exploring ways to make his dream more secure, possibly going back to school for a better-paying job or finding an existing organization to finance his dream.

What if you feel woefully underqualified for the kind of job you dream about?

In *Careering and Re-careering for the 1990s* Ronald L. Krannich identifies the following as job market "myth no. 6": "Employers hire the best qualified candidates—those with the most education, skills, and experience. Without a great deal of experience and numerous qualifications, I don't have a chance." The surprising reality, says Krannich, is this:

Employers seldom hire the best qualified individual because "qualifications" are difficult to measure. Employers normally seek *competent, intelligent, honest, and likeable* individuals—qualities that cannot be communicated effectively on application forms and résumés. . . . If, for example, employers only hired on the basis of education, skills, and experience, they would not need to interview candidates. Such static information is available in applications and résumés. Employers interview because they want to see a warm body—how you look and interact with them and how you will fit into their organization.[12] (Emphasis added)

Keep Your Perspective

There is another aspect to this dreaming that we need to remember. Even if we envision the perfect job, and even if we find it, that does not mean we have reached heaven and will be totally fulfilled forever. Losing a job can reopen our dreams; it can also show us that our jobs are not God's total provision for our happiness.

Linda Schimke was looking forward to a promotion when her job with AT&T was eliminated. She found another job, but her attitude toward work has changed significantly: "I want to do the best job I can, but at the same time I am making much more of an effort to have a fuller personal life. I used to get most of my satisfaction from my job. But I have learned that a company can't give you your whole life."[13]

"For every woman who craves the status of an executive," wrote George Will in 1978, "there is an executive who would, if he could, flee to northern Minnesota and open a bait-and-tackle shop."[14] Northern Wisconsin and northern Minnesota have certain similarities, and we know several urban executives who successfully fled their high-status, high-pressure careers. Up here the woods are full of them (literally), and they wouldn't go back for anything.

Our dreams for our lives can be an opening for the voice of God, but we are still fallen people. Our dreams will be flawed and tarnished because we, the dreamers, are sinners. Our dreams can be selfish and deceptive. We must want for ourselves what God wants for us and nothing more. As in every other area of our lives, in our work we must pray, "Not my will, but yours be done."

Gary Hardaway was standing at a half-open door, careerwise, when he wrote about his potential "dream" situation. He says, "I have applied for a unique position, perhaps the ideal ministry for me. I have never wanted anything like I want this. If the Lord allows me to be selected, I can envision staying in this role for life. Never before could I say that."

The catch is that there were fifty applicants for Hardaway's "dream" ministry job, and only one opening. As he waited to hear, he was sharply aware that "in the end, only one dream will survive." He continued, "We all know that God's will is good, acceptable, and perfect. Yet 49 of us will have to believe that with a lump in our throats and a pain in our solar plexus."

There were no guarantees that what Hardaway wanted for himself would happen. He reminded himself—and us:

Setting goals is a dangerous thing. Having fervent dreams is even riskier. Few goals can be achieved by oneself. Often the outcome depends not only on our commitment, ability, and diligence, but also on someone else's opinion of us. It depends on reaction, events, circumstances—factors beyond our control.[16]

Gary Hardaway wrote that article in 1986. We never learned whether he got his dream job. Perhaps he got it, only to discover that it wasn't exactly what he had imagined. That's what happened to Derek.

Derek had a sales career going when the Lord called him to overseas missions. He was accepted into missionary training. Then, out of the blue, he was offered his "dream job" in sales. The money and status appealed to Derek too much to turn it down. He moved his family halfway across the country. (When we asked his wife if she went along with his decision, she replied, "I had to. All my stuff was in the U-Haul.") Derek reported for work at his "perfect" job. Two days later, he realized it was the biggest mistake he had ever made. He stuck it out for two miserable years before beginning over at the process of becoming a missionary.

At the beginning of this chapter we quoted Blair, who thanks God for the day he got fired. Robert does too, in a different way. When Robert saw that he would not be going back to his teaching job, he felt a lot of uncertainty about God's direction for his

future. He says, "I asked myself, 'What does the Lord have for
me? What am I doing with my life?' I found myself lacking a
major goal to be working toward. I would ask, 'Why doesn't God
write this on a wall so I can see it?' "

Time has given Robert a different perspective. He's now
working a job some would call underemployment for a teacher—a job we'll discuss in more detail in chapter seven. But at
a deeper level his view of himself has changed: "I still want God
to show me this great wonderful thing 'out there' that I'm supposed to be working toward. But God sees this wonderful person 'here' that he's working *with*. It's who I am, not what I
accomplish."

The abilities God gives us will never be as important as his
character-building inside us, regardless of whether our dreams
of work ever come to fruition or not. Still, it's nice when they
do.

Things to Do
☐ Brainstorm the things you'd love to do or always dreamed
of doing.
☐ Identify your heroes.
☐ Consider what your "gifted passion" might be. Ask other
people's opinions and listen with an open mind. Pray that the
Lord will show you (or confirm if you already know) what it is.
☐ Take skills-identifying or gifts-identifying tests.

Suggested Reading
Bolles, Richard N. *What Color Is Your Parachute?* Berkeley, Calif.:
Ten Speed Press. This helpful book is published annually.
Get the latest edition you can find.
————. *The New Quick Job-Hunting Map: How to Create a Pic-
ture of Your Ideal Job or Next Career.* Berkeley, Calif.: Ten Speed
Press, 1990. A small book of skill-discovery exercises excerpt-
ed from *What Color Is Your Parachute?*

Crystal, John C., and Richard N. Bolles. *Where Do I Go from Here with My Life?* Berkeley, Calif.: Ten Speed Press, 1974.

Dell, Twyla. *An Honest Day's Work: Motivating Employees to Give Their Best.* Los Altos, Calif.: Crisp Publications, 1988. Although it's written for employers, this interesting workbook will help you understand why you thrive—or feel stifled—in particular work situations.

Harris, Janis Long. *Secrets of People Who Love Their Work.* Downers Grove, Ill.: InterVarsity Press, 1992. Stories of contemporary people who are happy in their work, how they got there, and how they stay that way.

Pearson, Henry G. *Your Hidden Skills: Clues to Careers and Future Pursuits.* Wayland, Mass.: Mowry Press, 1981.

Saltzman, Amy, Mary Lord, and Edward C. Baig. "Voices from the Front." *U.S. News & World Report,* January 13, 1992.

6

Beyond the End of Your Rope: A Guide to Other Resources

*When a person finally gets a job,
it's in the dumbest way or the easiest way possible.
But everything up to that point is hard.*
Gary, experienced job-finder

*Let the morning bring me word of your unfailing love,
for I have put my trust in you.
Show me the way I should go,
for to you I lift up my soul.*
Psalm 143:8

Where do you go from here?

You've decided what you like to do and the skills you possess. You've reconsidered your goals and maybe you've established a new direction for the career you want to pursue.

You've answered the newspaper want ads, talked to the people at Job Service, filled out application forms, perhaps had some interviews. You've exhausted all your leads. It begins to look like there's no job available for you.

Above all you want to believe it's not hopeless. There must be some employer out there somewhere who at this moment is searching for somebody just like you—somebody with your unique combination of skills and interests. Sympathetic friends tell you to buck up: "There's still hope." But you need more than general expressions of confidence. You want to know—specifically and clearly—how do you find that person out there who is looking for you and doesn't know it?

What About God's Will?

If only God would tell us, at moments like this, exactly what is going to happen. Or at least what's going on. We could stand to wait for the right job if we knew for sure it was coming. But are we on the wrong track? Are we pursuing something that isn't God's will? Will we be jobless one more week? One more day? One more year?

Most of us don't expect to see our fate written across the sky, but we believe that if we go ahead in faith and pursue what seems right, the Lord will guide us to the place he wants us. Yet the time comes when circumstances seem to contradict our conviction.

We've pursued a particular job which seemed made for us. The door was closed in our faces. That has happened again and yet again. We've wasted days and weeks pursuing situations that didn't work out. Is God going to tell us what to do or isn't he?

Elisabeth Elliot recalls two adventurous Americans who arrived in Quito, Ecuador, headed for the deep rain forest to write a book about their experiences. They asked her, the local missionary, to give them a few useful Indian phrases to help them get by.

They described their equipment to me with great pride, and I could see that it was not going to be of much use. I wanted to tell them that what they ought to have was a guide, but they had asked only for help on the language and not for advice. So off they went, full of confidence. Perhaps they found their way all right, survived, and even wrote the book. I never heard of them again.

We sometimes come to God for guidance, Elisabeth Elliot says, much like those two adventurers came to her, "confident and, we think, well-informed and well-equipped. . . . We know what we need—a yes or no answer, please, to a simple question. Or perhaps a road sign. Something quick and easy to point the way. What we really ought to have is the Guide himself."[1]

Times of confusion over God's will can be times of strengthening and deepening our relationship with God himself—with no demand for knowing what's coming tomorrow or even what we should do tomorrow. Through his anger over the loss of his job, Norm began to come face to face with a God who simply is—rather than demanding that the Lord do certain things for him. He explains: "After I lost my job I was angry with God, and that's a problem for a Christian because you're not 'supposed' to be angry with God. But God *is*—he'll be here when I'm gone, and he loves me. I don't understand his love, but he's told me to rest in it."

At the same time, the Lord is our Shepherd and does promise to guide us. Deeply committed Christians who truly want to find God's will often go through great anxiety when job hunting because they're afraid of "missing it." If they do something wrong, if they don't detect God's voice at exactly the right time, they'll blow it and always have to settle for his second best for their lives.

The evidence of the Bible is that the Lord can and does speak clearly when he wants us to do something specific, and he'll protect us from foolish choices when we rely on him. So we keep going, trusting we're led by our guide.

Doing the Groundwork

Who? What? Where? When? How? Like a term paper, finding out about jobs is basically a research project. We need information. We want reliable facts. Our best approach is the same way we approached our term papers.

Or, should we say, the way we should have approached our term papers? We all remember those nights before a paper was due, staying up all night typing page after page off the top of our heads, hoping it made sense. Usually the paper—and our grade—reflected our failure to do the necessary research. A job search which fails to first do the necessary research will probably flunk just as soundly.

Assuming we went about our research paper the right way, what did we do? We started by going to the library and looking up pertinent subjects in the card catalog. When we couldn't find what we needed there, we started asking people for help. If we were really beginning in the dark about the subject, we first consulted people to ask what we should look for in the card catalog. For our job search as for our term papers, written resources and live human beings are still our best sources of information.

If you're put off by the "term paper" comparison, then think up your own metaphor for a process which is fun, challenging, and within your control. One writer compares it to a detective solving a mystery:

Detective work is a state of mind. Once you adopt this attitude, you will regard your career as a complicated mystery story and become absorbed in following the clues and looking for new evidence; you will enjoy being the Perry Mason of your own career.[2]

Whatever you call it, just don't think of it as a guessing game or a game of chance!

Not everybody realizes that the search for the right job in the right place is first of all a search for information. When Victor lost his executive job, he assumed that another position would turn up soon, and he was soon disappointed. He learned the hard way: "Nobody told me I had to spend time investigating a lot of things. Nobody told me you don't get that much done in one interview."

Fortunately, in any community there are people whose job, whose life work, whose calling and love is to help you find the information you need. These people are called *librarians*. Get to know yours.

We live in a town of about 9,000 in a remote and economically depressed area 70 miles from a medium-sized city and 150 miles from a major city. Our public library does not have a lavish budget or grand facilities. Still, we found almost all the resources for this book through our library. There are several shelves of books on careers and job-hunting, most of them published quite recently.

You aren't limited to what you find on the shelves. If a particular book isn't in our library, the staff can often find it through statewide interlibrary loan. They can also do an interlibrary search for particular topics—say, outdoor careers. Besides the old-fashioned card catalog, we can sit down and use the computerized "card catalog" to search topics, titles and authors in several libraries in our area.

If you live in a community with a college, technical school, or university, their libraries are also available to you. Feel free to use them.

We hope your local library is already familiar and friendly territory. If you still imagine the library as a silence-shrouded place where a drab person behind a desk peers at you censoriously, ready to say "Shhhhh!"—well, if that image was ever true, it isn't true now.

In fact libraries are filled with so much freely available information, and the people who work there are so willing to help, that you may feel overwhelmed. We were when we began research for this book and specifically for this chapter.

We can't begin to condense or even list all the job-hunting resources available. Instead, in this chapter we will go through (in reasonably chronological order) the process by which you can find and use your available job-information resources.

We'll steer you to sources we found particularly sensible and readable, particularly if they are repeatedly cited in other works and include bibliographies of further resources. (We'll refer only to titles and authors; see the Suggested Reading sections at the end of each chapter for full citations.)

General Job-Search Guides
Perhaps you've already consulted the most famous book on job-hunting, *What Color Is Your Parachute?* Richard N. Bolles self-published it at his local photocopy shop in 1970. From that "first edition" of 200 copies, it is now published annually and has sold in the millions. If you were to buy only one book on finding a job, this would be a good selection.

The focus of *What Color Is Your Parachute?* is not the job market, but the job-hunter. Bolles's premise is that you can and should take control of your job-hunt—but first you must "do some homework on yourself" to discover the "what, where, and how" of the job that will be most fulfilling. The bulk of the book is self-discovery exercises to answer those three questions.

Especially intriguing to Christians is Bolles's appendix on "Religion and Job-Hunting: How to Find Your Mission in Life." He insists that job-hunting cannot be separated from our calling from God. We won't take the space here to critique Bolles's theology, but his article is a refreshing change from a secular materialistic approach to job-hunting.

Lacking the graphics and cleverness of *What Color Is Your Parachute?* but excellent in a different way is Howard Figler's *The Complete Job-Search Handbook.* Figler helps you develop twenty career-search skills in four basic categories: self-assessment, detective (research), communication, and selling yourself. He also discusses special problems such as ways job-hunters foil themselves and how to get experience through alternative forms of work.

Career Research

Before committing yourself too firmly to any particular career, it is wise to give some thought to whether that career has a future. The much-valued MBA of the 1980s, for example, has lost much of its luster in the 1990s. Two books which may help avoid career-choice dead ends are *Careering and Re-careering for the 1990's* (Ronald L. Krannich) and *Work in the New Economy* (Robert Wegmann, Robert Chapman and Miriam Johnson). The first part of each book analyzes today's changing economy and job market. Both books have extensive projections of the trends in various occupations.

Interviewing for Information

What if you've narrowed your focus to a particular career path you want to pursue, but you don't know what companies or organizations employ people doing that particular work? Every book on finding a job will tell you how to go about "interviewing for information"—that is, exploratory talks with people in various careers to find out how and whether your skills fit those careers. In *The Complete Job-Search Handbook,* Howard Figler defines five "levels" of informational interviews:

Level 1: Background research on a field of work
Level 2: Researching a type of organization
Level 3: Finding out where the jobs might be
Level 4: Exploring a particular organization
Level 5: Talking with decision makers[3]

When we're interviewing many people "just to find out" abo't their businesses, obviously we'll sometimes find ourselves talking with someone who could hire us. Figler counsels honesty in those situations:

Don't play the hidden agenda game. Don't ask to see people on pretense of wanting information and advice, when you are sneakily trying to edge close and ask for a job. This tactic insults the other person and may haunt you for the remainder of your job search. Let the interview be a pleasant and nonthreatening one. If the person volunteers information about job leads, that is so much gravy for you, but not something you asked for.[4]

Networking

"It's not what you know, it's who you know." Most of us don't like that truism, but when it comes to job-hunting, it's generally accurate. Though "networking" has become a trite term for "contacting everybody who can help you or who might know somebody who can help you," it is still a valuable means of finding a job.

Most firms can fill a large proportion of their openings from the two groups of applicants who regularly approach them. The first group come *recommended by friends, relatives and present employees.* The second come in on their own initiative.[5]

Like it or not, most jobs are found through "knowing somebody"—through the advice and knowledge of friends or relatives, or their friends and relatives. "Since the 1930s studies of blue-collar, white-collar, managerial, technical, and professional workers have found that . . . from 60 to 90 percent of jobs are found informally—mainly through friends, relatives, and direct contacts."[6]

The trouble is often we just don't feel like talking about the ugly—and embarrassing—fact that we're out of work. But it makes good sense to start telling everybody you can about your need of a new job. Why miss any opportunity of talking to that one person who knows about a place you can fill?

Don Double of Career Transition Consultants in Chicago advised a laid-off manager to let everyone know he was looking for work: "By limiting the number of people who know you're out of work, you've cut out your best tool—personal contacts. Make it your goal to reach 60 people within eight weeks. Two-thirds of all positions are filled through contacts."[7]

We appreciate the emphasis on ethics and honesty in Ronald and Caryl Rae Krannich's *Network Your Way to Job & Career Success*. It's a clear step-by-step guide to developing and using personal contacts while acknowledging the limitations and abuses of "networking."

You can start the process by making a list of anybody and everybody who might possibly help you in your search for a job. That means more than your immediate friends and acquaintances. It means people you haven't contacted for a while but whom you can still reach: old friends, workmates, schoolmates, former employers. Don't forget former business contacts, sales representatives, buyers, technical people. They don't even have to be people who immediately remember your name.

In a study of professionals who had recently changed jobs, Mark Granovetter, author of *Getting a Job*, discovered an important pattern. Many did get their new positions with the help of personal contacts. However, a large proportion of these contacts were people they didn't know very well. Often those who helped them were met by chance, had not been seen for months, and had never been particularly close friends. Yet they provided the information that led to a new job. Granovetter was so struck by this pattern that he called it "the strength of weak ties."[8]

Gary, our aspiring artist friend, has filled the gaps in his artistic career with various jobs. He says talking to people is vital to his frequent job-hunting successes:

I let people know I'm looking for a job, just like if I was looking for a car or an apartment. Sometimes I'm scared to do it because of the fear of rejection, but the best thing to do is keep doing it. I rarely find work in the "conventional" way—not through newspapers or job service—but through running into people. That's how I got started working in community support with disabled people, which is what I'm doing now.

If you find it hard to keep contacting people informally on your own, consider getting together with several other job seekers for mutual encouragement. We'll discuss such support groups more fully in chapter nine.

If you are involved in a Bible study group or Sunday-school class, you'll find that to be a good resource of contacts. You already know the people, and they're already supportive of you. Perhaps you shy away from "using" your Christian friends in this way, and it's wise to be cautious about motives. A Bible study group is not there solely to help us find work. Certainly, we shouldn't start going to a Bible study purely to get contacts for a job hunt. But as long as they're people you already know and trust, give them the opportunity to help you.

There is a certain point when "networking" can become discouraging. It comes when one more person gets out one more scrap of paper to write one more name and phone number of "somebody you really ought to talk to." At that moment you'll realize how many of those scraps of paper you've collected, and you'll wonder why this person won't magically solve your problem. Well, take the piece of paper graciously anyway. People want to help, and who knows where it may lead?

Other people are a tremendous resource and a gift from God, but we can't expect them to assume responsibility for finding us a job. Howard Figler cautions: "Contacts are necessary to any effective job search, but you cannot build an entire strategy around them." He continues:

> Networking functions best when it is part of a daily routine, not when it is used all at once and must be the burden of a hurry-up job search. Too much reliance upon contacts can become offensive to those who are being tapped. A personal referral network should occur naturally, not by brute force.[9]

Approaching the Employer
In *What Color Is Your Parachute?* Richard Bolles calls this stage

the "how" phase of the job hunt. After you've identified several employment targets that stand out above all the rest, the questions facing you are three "how" questions:

1. HOW do I find out who has the power to hire me there?
2. HOW do I get in for a job interview with that person?
3. HOW do I convince them that they should hire me?[10]

In this age of video, it's good to remember that paper and the printed word still pack a powerful punch. Your prospective employer's first hint of your existence is likely to be your letter or résumé, or both. Unless they are grabbers and connect your skills to the business's needs, they may be the last the employer sees of you.

Two helpful resources in workbook format are *Dynamite Cover Letters & Other Great Job Search Letters* and *High Impact Resumes & Letters*. Both books get right down to business demonstrating how to put your message on paper effectively. Some sample advice:

Job search letters should be written according to key principles of good advertising copy. They should include the following principles:

Catch the reader's attention. . . . Persuade the reader about you, the product . . . by stressing value and benefits. . . . Convince the reader with more evidence. . . . Move the reader to take action (acquire the product).[11]

Most other job-hunting books include chapters on résumé and cover-letter writing. Occasionally the advice is contradictory, but most of it follows the principles just stated.

The Interview

Your foot is finally in the door. Your interview is scheduled and you're anticipating it with that dizzy mixture of hope and dread. The Scouts' old motto holds true here: "Be Prepared." Richard Bolles writes:

You sell yourself by finding out as much about that organization as you possibly can before you ever go in there for an interview. . . . How much information should you gather? If possible, more than you are ever going to have to use, at least during the hiring interview. But the depth of your research will pay off in the quiet sense of confidence you exude.[12]

If you need information about your prospective employer in a hurry, a particularly valuable book is Mary Ellen Templeton's *Help! My Job Interview Is Tomorrow!* As the panicky title implies, it's a step-by-step workbook for using the library to research an employer. Of course, it would be equally useful in nonemergency situations.

"In every job interview," writes Howard Figler, "there is a hidden agenda of nine items, regardless of the nature of the work or the type of company." He assures us, "It's less confusing than you think. When the interviewer asks a question and you answer it, you're often covering several factors at the same time." The nine factors are:

1. Personal impression
2. Competence
3. Likability
4. Motivation/enthusiasm/commitment
5. Leadership
6. Communication skills
7. Poise and maturity
8. Outside interests
9. Your relationships[13]

If the process of "selling yourself" in an interview were reduced to a single, central element, it would be this: "You must help the interviewer see that you have potential for performing the present job well, by showing him/her something you have done or learned before that provides clues to your potential."[14]

Things to Do
☐ Continue to pray for the Lord's guidance.

□ Let anybody and everybody know you are looking for work.
□ Go to libraries and read all you can about the field(s) of work which interest you.
□ Talk to people who are doing, or who know about, the work which interests you.
□ Research specific employers who are hiring in that field.
□ When you approach employers, present yourself on paper attractively and professionally.
□ Before you go into a job interview, prepare thoroughly.

Suggested Reading

Elliot, Elisabeth. *A Slow and Certain Light.* Waco, Tex.: Word, 1973. A small but profound book about how Christians are guided by the living God. Explores the conditions, objectives and means of God's guidance.

Friesen, Garry, with J. Robin Maxson. *Decision Making and the Will of God.* Portland, Ore.: Multnomah Press, 1980. Makes a well-reasoned challenge to the "bull's-eye" theory of God's guidance, presenting the "way of wisdom" as an alternative.

Krannich, Ronald L., and William J. Banis. *High Impact Resumes & Letters: How to Communicate Your Qualifications to Employers.* Woodbridge, Va.: Impact Publications, 1990. Develops the reason behind résumés and letters, then gives a wealth of "how-to" information. Includes a topical bibliography of career resources.

Krannich, Ronald L., and Caryl Rae Krannich. *Dynamite Cover Letters & Other Great Job Search Letters.* Woodbridge, Va.: Impact Publications, 1992. A practical workbook on "the power of paper"—not only cover letters but approach letters, résumés, follow-up letters, and thank-yous.

Quinn, Jane Bryant. "Self-Help for the Jobless." *Newsweek,* Dec. 16, 1991, p. 52. Newsweek's financial columnist writes about support groups for job seekers in places such as Westminster Presbyterian Church in Wilmington, Delaware, and Marble

Collegiate Church in New York.

Templeton, Mary Ellen. *Help! My Job Interview Is Tomorrow! How to Use the Library to Research an Employer.* New York: Neal-Schuman Publishers, Inc., 1991. A step-by-step guide, in workbook form, for uncovering information about a prospective employer. Written by a university librarian. Includes bibliography of hundreds of business directories.

Wegmann, Robert, and Robert Chapman. *The Right Place at the Right Time.* Berkeley, Calif.: Ten Speed Press, 1990.

Wegmann, Robert, Robert Chapman, and Miriam Johnson. *Work in the New Economy: Careers and Job Seeking into the 21st Century.* Rev. ed. Indianapolis, Ind.: JIST Works, 1989. How work is changing and how to cope with the changes. "Highly highly recommended" by job-search dean Richard Bolles.

7

Making the Best
of Underemployment

Sometimes I think "I'm in my 40s now—
how come I'm not I'm further ahead?
How come my classmates are doing so much better than I am?"
Robert, former teacher

Whatever you do, work at it with all your heart,
as working for the Lord, not for men,
since you know you will receive an inheritance
from the Lord as a reward.
It is the Lord Christ you are serving.
Colossians 3:23-24

Let's say a job comes my way at last. It's real work for real
money. It's open to me if I want it. The problem is . . .
I'm a skilled machinist, and this is a job clerking in a
convenience store. Or I'm a computer technician and this is
assembly-line work. Or I have twelve years of teaching experience and this is a job as a teacher's aide—for a first-year teacher fresh out of graduate school!

For some people being underemployed means "I'm not being paid what I'm worth." For others it means "I'm working far
below my capabilities." For others, underemployment means
"I'm not using my education."

There are times when, to put it bluntly, our underemployment is our own fault. We're stuck in an inferior job because

we haven't taken the initiative to find something better or to get ourselves qualified for something better.

Lyn, who found herself out of work when her store closed, regrets that she didn't take advantage of a government job-training program:

I keep saying "I should have" and "I'm kicking myself." CEP [Concentrated Employment Program] would have paid for my retraining, but I didn't take it. I could have taken courses for nurses' aide or for certified child care. I didn't do any of it. I was afraid that even if I trained for a new job, prospective employers would say "no experience."

Deciding Which Way to Go

Sometimes people stay underemployed because they can't (or won't) make up their minds which career they want to pursue. There's Lonnie, for example, who insists, "I can do anything. Anything." What is he doing? Not much. Clerking here and there in convenience stores. "For right now," he says, "I'm just surviving day-to-day."

In Sylvia Plath's novel *The Bell Jar,* the star graduate of an exclusive women's college finds herself with no more awards and prizes to win. After years of being told that she's full of promise and can accomplish anything, she sits at home doing nothing. She imagines a great tree from which many branches are growing, laden with all kinds of fruit, while she sits in the crotch of the tree, starving to death because she can't make up her mind which fruit to pick.

Ray, in his thirties, is working in a fast-food place. He is an intelligent and articulate person who started college but never finished. "I think about what I'd like to do," he says, "but there are so many things I could do, and I think, how would I ever decide?" Ray is sitting in the tree considering all the different fruits. For now he has made his decision to decide for none of them, and he remains drastically underemployed.

Who Is Underemployed?

Ray's underemployment is obvious. There are other people who seem to be doing fine on the outside but feel underemployed on the inside.

Victor, a former executive, now operates his own retail business, which most of us would consider a respectable and even enviable position. Still he admits he goes to his college alumni gatherings with mixed feelings. "I want to see the people, but I don't want to be asked, 'What have you been doing the past years?' I don't think operating my business sounds good enough."

When it comes to "working beneath ourselves," as we interviewed people and examined our own experience, we came to the conclusion that *underemployment is more a state of mind than a condition of circumstances.* There may be no official definition of underemployment, but if you feel underemployed, you are. The good news is on the flip side of that. Not everybody who looks underemployed on the outside feels that way on the inside.

If you define underemployment in purely financial terms, in our area of the country we are surrounded by underemployed people, and a lot of them are underemployed on purpose. Many left well-paying jobs in the city to live up here because they like the atmosphere. Others graduated from the local college with environmental-science degrees and are sticking around the area to stay close to nature. These people are working at whatever jobs they can find in order to live here. Some have had to start their own businesses; others work at jobs quite unrelated to their education and training. Are those people underemployed?

Financially, yes. Emotionally, no. Financially, many people would consider us underemployed. We could have made more money working full-time as a carpenter/handyman and secretary. As writers, we have not enjoyed great monetary success.

Yet we both considered ourselves far more "underemployed" as handyman and secretary and would consider it a step down to go back to that.

Paul's Example

Underemployment is more subjective than it seems at first. We wonder, what would be the opinion of the most famous "underemployed" person of the New Testament (other than the Son of God working as a carpenter)—the apostle Paul?

Saul of Tarsus was highly qualified for the job of chief first-century missionary to the Roman Empire. He was intelligent, well-educated in religious matters, single-minded, tough, articulate. He was the last person we would have recruited for the job, but God thought he was the ideal candidate.

Saul had earned such a reputation as a persecutor of Christians that Ananias, the man sent to baptize him, was terrified even to meet him. Yet when Saul was on the way to Damascus to arrest more Christians, he was literally knocked down in his tracks and told that Christ had selected him to be "my chosen instrument to carry my name before the Gentiles and their kings and before the people of Israel" (Acts 9:15). Any Christian would be honored to have such a career.

Paul, as Saul became known, spent several intense years in the work of itinerant evangelism and teaching. After a dramatic encounter with pagan worshippers in Athens, he went to the city of Corinth. There his career took a surprising turn toward the mundane:

> There he met a Jew named Aquila, a native of Pontus, who had recently come from Italy with his wife Priscilla, because Claudius had ordered all the Jews to leave Rome. Paul went to see them, and because he was a tentmaker as they were, he stayed and worked with them. Every Sabbath he reasoned in the synagogue, trying to persuade Jews and Greeks. (Acts 18:2-4)

Tents at that time were made of goats'-hair cloth, which Bedouin Arabs still use for the purpose. It's possible Paul was making leather items rather than tents, because the word translated "tentmaker" may also mean "leatherworker."[1] Regardless of the product Paul manufactured, the work was a long way from preaching and teaching. The work was also a long way from Paul's education. In the Jewish educational system of those days, Paul had done postdoctoral work. He had been thoroughly trained in the Jewish Law by the revered rabbi Gamaliel (Acts 22:3). Gamaliel was the first rabbi to be given the title "Rabban" ("our Master, our Great One") rather than the ordinary "Rabbi" ("my Master").[2] Paul described himself as "advancing in Judaism beyond many Jews of my own age" (Galatians 1:14).

Now imagine Paul sitting in his workshop six days a week. It's hardly our popular image of the great apostle. We see him in Athens, standing in the midst of the Areopagus proclaiming the one true God. Or perhaps we think of him penning a personal letter to his young friend Timothy, or standing in chains before Agrippa, or giving courage to sailors in a storm at sea. But sneezing at goat's hair and pricking his fingers with a sewing needle? Getting out to evangelize only on the sabbath? What a comedown for the apostle Paul! Or was it?

Writing some time later to Christians who were the fruit of his ministry in Corinth, Paul reminded them that he had the right to expect them to support him financially.

> Who serves as a soldier at his own expense? Who plants a vineyard and does not eat of its grapes? Who tends a flock and does not drink of the milk? . . . If we have sown spiritual seed among you, is it too much if we reap a material harvest from you? . . . The Lord has commanded that those who preach the gospel should receive their living from the gospel. (1 Corinthians 9:7-8, 11, 14)

Paul chose to support himself by working at a trade rather than burden the young church. Perhaps he also enjoyed the change of pace from the mental and verbal work of evangelizing and teaching. We don't know all his reasons for working as a tentmaker in Corinth. We know more about Paul's reasons for working in the city of Thessalonica, where he and Silas later won converts to Christ. In Thessalonica, Paul and his companions worked in order to set an example. Some of the Thessalonian believers had a problem with laziness. Toward the end of his life he reminded the Christians there:

> We were not idle when we were with you, nor did we eat anyone's food without paying for it. On the contrary, we worked night and day, laboring and toiling so that we would not be a burden to any of you. We did this, not because we do not have the right to such help, but in order to make ourselves a model for you to follow. For even when we were with you, we gave you this rule: "If a man will not work, he shall not eat."
>
> We hear that some among you are idle. They are not busy; they are busybodies. Such people we command and urge in the Lord Jesus Christ to settle down and earn the bread they eat. (2 Thessalonians 3:7-12)

In both Corinth and Thessalonica, Paul could have resented his "underemployment." He might have thought: "If only those Corinthians had more money to give . . . If only those Thessalonians would get off their rear ends and take some responsibility for themselves . . . Don't they know I've got more important things to do than sit in this musty workshop all week?"

What About Us?

The evidence is that Paul took on his tentmaking willingly. We would consider him underemployed, but he didn't think of himself that way. Well, that was a fine choice for Paul, but what about those of us who have underemployment forced on us? We have to do this nothing job just to survive. Its mindless routine and Mickey-Mouse triviality insult our intelligence, education and creativity. We feel like slaves.

For that matter, we can feel like underemployed slaves in a "good" job. Maybe we're slaves to the lender because we got ourselves too deeply into debt. Our "good" job helps us pay the credit card bills, but the paycheck isn't sufficient compensation for the soul-deadening nature of the job.

The Scripture at the beginning of this chapter was written to underemployed people. Paul wrote it to slaves—literally—people forced to do the most menial tasks with no choice in the matter. Certainly, he felt some kinship with them. His instructions to slaves are good instructions to any worker, but they especially fit one who feels put upon and trivialized by underemployment.

This Scripture gives us hope that even dead-end or mind-numbing jobs can be taken out of the mundane and infused with meaning. It tells us that there is something good in faithfully performing even petty or monotonous work, because we are really working not for people but for the Lord.

Working for the Lord? That's what pastors and missionaries do, right? How is a guy with a master's degree "working for the Lord" when he's stacking oranges in a grocery store because he can't find a teaching job? How is a talented artist "working for the Lord" when she's pasting up ads in a small-town newspaper because she can't make a living as a sculptor?

In his New Testament paraphrase, the British writer and pastor J. B. Phillips put it this way:

Slaves, your job is to obey your human masters, not with the idea of catching their eye or currying favour, but as a sincere expression of your devotion to the Lord. Whatever your task is, put your whole heart and soul into it, as into work done for the Lord and not merely for men—knowing that your real reward will come from him. You are actually slaves of the Lord Christ Jesus. (Colossians 3:22-24)

It's hard to imagine our teacher and artist putting their "whole heart and soul" into stacking those oranges and pasting up those ads. It's hard to imagine a computer technician putting his or her "whole heart and soul" into pulling the same lever all day on an assembly line, especially if it's to make some unnecessary consumer gizmo. Surely it's asking too much for all those people to throw their "whole heart and soul" into that kind of work for the sake of the work itself.

But notice this. Scripture does not ask us to do it for the work's sake. It asks us to do it for the Lord's sake, because we are really working for him.

Suddenly another dimension has entered our dull "nothing" job. As soon as the living God is involved in something, it immediately becomes bigger than we are. Now there's more going on than pulling that lever, stacking those oranges, or pasting up those ads. What does it mean to work for the Lord? At the most superficial level, this Scripture means the Lord is our real "boss."

Working for the Lord

Sandy once worked in a government office with a fellow who tended to lounge around and work as little as possible. Every time the boss walked through the room, this guy would pick up the phone and start dialing or pick up a legal pad and start scribbling. He wasn't calling anybody in particular or writing anything special, but did he ever look busy! That person's "work" was a perfect example of what the Bible calls by the picturesque word "eyeservice" (Colossians 3:22 and Ephesians 6:6 RSV). The Greek word is *ophthalmodoulia:* "service performed only under the master's eye (*ophthalmos,* an eye, *doulos,* a slave), diligently performed when he is looking, but neglected in his absence."[3]

That fellow got away with it—and do we dare to admit, we all get away with it—because our human bosses can't keep their eyes on us all day. God, however, is always watching. Our work is always on display before him.

Now that's God-as-boss on the crassest level. If that's how we understand "working for the Lord," then he's only a celestial Santa Claus: "He sees you when you're sleeping, he knows when you're awake, he knows if you've been bad or good, so be good for goodness' sake!"

Still the fact that God sees us is something to think about, because underemployment tempts us to *ophthalmodoulia*. Since we don't really want to be there, we're usually not committed to doing the best job possible. So God is our boss. But there's more to it than that. For a Christian there is a far deeper and warmer meaning to being "slaves of the Lord Christ Jesus."

Paul the apostle/tentmaker opened several of his letters with the greeting, "Paul, a servant of Christ Jesus" or "a servant of God" (Romans 1:1, Philippians 1:1, Titus 1:1). The word is *doulos*, which could also be translated "slave." Paul had a tremendous certainty that he was working for the Lord and that the Lord had chosen him for the particular job he was doing. He was absolutely convinced that God "set me apart from birth and called me by his grace" and "was pleased to reveal his Son in me so that I might preach him among the Gentiles" (Galatians 1:15-16). Without such a driving sense of purpose, it's hard to imagine Paul lasting through his imprisonments, beatings, shipwreck, hunger, sleeplessness and constant danger (2 Corinthians 11:23-28).

Seeing the Opportunities

What difference would it make to carry such a sense of purpose into our underemployment? How will that "nothing" job change if we believe that Christ has carefully and deliberately put us there for now, right there in that Mickey-Mouse job, not because he wants to treat us badly, but for his own purposes?

Our job, no matter how "small" it is, then becomes full of

opportunities. They're not opportunities as the world thinks of opportunities. They're probably not opportunities to get ahead in the world or to fulfill the career we dream of; they're opportunities of a different kind. Jesus said that no matter what our situation, we are to serve as his agents for change:

You are the salt of the earth. But if the salt loses its saltiness, how can it be made salty again? It is no longer good for anything, except to be thrown out and trampled by men.

You are the light of the world. A city on a hill cannot be hidden. Neither do people light a lamp and put it under a bowl. Instead they put it on its stand, and it gives light to everyone in the house. In the same way, let your light shine before men, that they may see your good deeds and praise your Father in heaven. (Matthew 5:13-16)

Salt can be sprinkled anywhere. Light can shine anywhere. We are his agents even in situations where we're working far beneath our abilities and education. The word *tentmaking* has come down through Christian history as a term for "ordinary work done to support oneself while ministering." Dale found working as a handyman in the Chicago area to be a time of tentmaking. In the course of the work he also found he could be salt and light.

Because it was self-employment, the hours were flexible. That gave him greater opportunities to be involved with people, including students at Northwestern University. He treasured the experience of taking part in meetings and retreats with foreign students through the ministry of ISI (International Students, Inc.).

The time flexibility made ministry easier, but he found the work itself often became a source of ministry. By working alone and keeping his prices low, he was able to provide a much-needed service for several widows in the neighborhood as he shoveled snow, repaired light fixtures, and fixed broken locks.

Dale grew up on a small, struggling farm where if something

needed to be done, they did it themselves, and if they didn't know how to do it, they figured it out. He used those skills when he adapted numerous common household items for the use of a quadriplegic man. After Dale modified one house for him, he sold that home and bought another, and he started over.

The work also led to interesting conversations. Tom, our quadriplegic friend, had a van which accommodated his wheelchair. Occasionally Dale would drive him to downtown Chicago or to the airport, and those trips together gave them some great opportunities to talk about the meaning of life.

Another time, when Dale was working in a home, a small boy took some electrical connectors to play with. At first he denied knowing where they were. When he finally told me he had taken them, that led us naturally to talk about why people are tempted to lie and how we need God's forgiveness. We had quite a talk while I finished installing the electrical outlets.

During part of that same time, Sandy was working temporary secretarial jobs. Financially, those jobs were not underemployment. For a writer, however, there's no worse underemployment than having to type somebody else's bad grammar. The redeeming factor of the work (other than the pay) was that it often became a channel of ministry.

Because her coworkers knew she would be there only a short while, they talked to her about all kinds of things—their families, their fears, what they really thought of working in that crummy place, and their spiritual beliefs. They felt safe opening up because in a week she'd be gone, so there were some great opportunities for witness. Sandy thinks she was probably more bold because in a week she knew she'd be gone!

Many women looking for work are still asked, "Can you type?" and written off if they can't. At a time when many women are underemployed, Jerry and Mary White's comments to working women are good for any of us:

Many jobs are routine to the point of monotony, offering

little or no opportunity for creativity.

One way to battle this disadvantage is to do the best possible work at all times, maintaining a standard of excellence that will provide a measure of challenge. Keep Colossians 3:23 continually in mind, making service to Christ the motive for your work.

More importantly, boredom frequently has a root of doubt and questioning whether we are in God's will. If you are convinced that God has directed you to work and has provided the job, you have a sense of purpose that will do much to eliminate boredom in even the most routine of jobs.[4]

Many Are Called
Underemployment isn't the best kind of employment, but we can find purpose in it if we surrender it to God's purposes and see the opportunities he brings our way through it. In Ben Patterson's words, "Mere jobs can become callings."

> Our English word *vocation* comes from the Latin word *vocare*, which means "to call." A vocation is literally a calling. . . . We Christians can have many different occupations, but just one vocation. Individually, we may be stone masons, accountants, psychologists or auto parts salespersons in our occupations. But we are all, each of us, called to be servants of Jesus Christ in our vocation.[5]

Robert works as a "job coach" for New Horizons North, a local organization which helps developmentally disabled people and people with mental illness work at jobs in the community and live independently. Robert had no previous experience working with disabled people; he got the job by answering a newspaper ad. Neither the pay nor the status of the job is very high.

Since Robert had taught in public schools and Christian schools, it would seem a comedown to spend the day teaching a mentally disabled person how to fold clothes or bag groceries. We talked with him partly to find out how he coped with underemployment, and his response was interesting: "I don't consider myself underemployed. I've liked this work very much. I like the contact with lots of interesting people, the day-to-day challenge of solving problems. My coworkers are a fine group of people to work with. There's no self-promotion."

Like Victor at his class reunions, Robert admits he sometimes compares himself unfavorably with his classmates. But he goes on to say, "If I'd been able to stay in teaching, I'd have a middle-class life but I don't think I'd be any happier."

The business which makes all this possible has an interesting history. New Horizons North was started in a church basement in 1968 by parents who wanted something meaningful for their adult disabled children to do. A large old building was purchased and became a "sheltered workshop" where disabled people worked at a recycling center, furniture refinishing shop, and resale shop as well as attending classes in everyday skills such as cooking, reading, handling money, grooming and current events. There were also several group homes where developmentally disabled people lived together.

A financial crisis in 1980 (when the bottom fell out of the recycling market) caused New Horizons North to reevaluate their mission. Diana Strzok, now director of New Horizons North, recalls, "After a lot of soul-searching and evaluation, we discovered that the people we served had become very dependent on us. We had been trying to 'be all things' to these people. We also realized that the sheltered workshop and group homes were isolating disabled people from the community. We stopped thinking that people with disabilities need to be cared for and 'kept busy,' and we started thinking that they need opportunities to do productive work—and can do it with support and training."

When local employers began to hire disabled people to work regular jobs, alongside them went nondisabled workers to help line up jobs, work alongside them for a while to teach them the jobs step-by-step, and help with special problems. They now employ dozens of nondisabled people who are very fulfilled— even if some would think them underemployed.

New Horizons North is an organization that shows how the roles of those who minister and those who are ministered to can become interchangeable. At the same time it turns the idea of meaningful employment on its head. Underemployment can be satisfying work.

Things to Do
☐ Name some unique opportunities you have had to serve the Lord in your present work.
☐ If you feel underemployed, look for ways that serving the Lord can bring new meaning to your work.
☐ Try to look at your work through Christ's eyes.

Suggested Reading
Patterson, Ben. *Work*. Downers Grove, Ill.: InterVarsity Press, 1992. Booklet adapted from chapters 1-4 of *The Grand Essentials*. Waco, Tex.: Word, 1987.
White, Jerry and Mary. *Your Job: Survival or Satisfaction? Christian Discipleship in a Secular Job*. Grand Rapids, Mich.: Zondervan, 1977.

8

Making Your
Own Way

"Say No to Real Jobs"
a T-shirt

She selects wool and flax
and works with eager hands.
She is like the merchant ships,
bringing her food from afar.
She gets up while it is still dark;
she provides food for her family
and portions for her servant girls.
She considers a field and buys it;
out of her earnings she plants a vineyard.
She sets about her work vigorously;
her arms are strong for her tasks.
She sees that her trading is profitable,
and her lamp does not go out at night.
Proverbs 31:13-18

I n the old British film *The Man in the White Suit* Alec Guinness, playing Sidney Stratton, invents the formula for an indestructible fabric. Nobody takes him seriously. As he sits dejected outside a textile factory, opportunity suddenly knocks: he is mistaken for a factory employee.

Sidney reports to "work" every day, using the factory to produce his miracle cloth. When his makeshift lab blows up, he leads the company bigwigs in a wild chase through the halls. They catch him and announce, "You're fired!" Sidney smugly replies, "You can't fire me, I don't work here!"

Such are the arrogant joys of self-employment! You may starve, but you can't be terminated.

Invent Your Own Job

We confess to a certain bias toward solving your unemployment problem by going to work for yourself. For most of twenty-two years we have been self-employed with a few periods of "regular" employment here and there. Writing full-time (more or less, with occasional bits of other self-employment), we have survived for twelve years.

Is this life for everybody? Emphatically, no. Is it for some people? Just as emphatically, yes. Whether you will make a good boss for yourself, we can't tell you. We can only give you some guidelines to help you know whether you'd be a good risk.

A lot of people are trying it—many, like us and maybe like you, because circumstances forced the choice on them. In 1991, 1.3 million new businesses opened their doors, more than half of them "sole proprietorships or microbusinesses with no more than two employees, typically operating out of a garage, basement or spare room."[1]

Just like Home

"Imagine working in a place where everyone treats you like family," says a recent magazine ad. Sure, who wouldn't want to work in a place like this? An attractive young couple in blue jeans lounge around an orderly desk. On the computer screen a chart goes up, up, up. There's a view of greenery through the French doors. On the desk there are samples of wallpaper borders which will decorate the office, the phone has one Post-it note stuck to it, and the friendly dog begs to be taken for a walk.

The message is clear: purchase this technology and enjoy a wonderful life working at home. Like most ads, it contains a mixture of truth and illusion.

Yes, when you work at home you can wear whatever you want (unless you greet customers and clients in your home/office).

Yes, your dog will be underfoot—not to mention your kids, door-to-door salespeople, and friends who assume that because you're home, you're "not busy."

No, your desk won't look like that. Nobody getting any serious work done at home has a desk as uncluttered as that one. And let's hope you have more than one phone message to return, or your business is pretty dead.

Yes, you'll be "treated like family," which often means you dispense with normal office politeness and grump at each other. After all, there's nobody to overhear you.

As for those wallpaper borders . . . they'll be lucky to get onto the walls because you're too busy *working* in your office to think of *decorating* your office.

In fact, for seven years the walls of our home office were papered in horrible orange-and-yellow flowers. They were that way when we moved in, and the only reason they got changed is that one day Sandy grabbed a peeling piece of wallpaper and ripped several yards of it off the wall. After that—unless we had wanted to work on the set of a Vincent Price movie—we had to do something.

Pros and Cons
Of all the careers you might jump into, self-employment deserves the most careful consideration and forethought. It is risky. No kidding. Self-employment does hold many pitfalls for the unprepared. But don't necessarily let its dangers keep you from starting your own business.

In *Start and Run a Profitable Home-Based Business*, Edna Sheedy lists advantages and disadvantages of working for yourself. So far we've found these to be accurate. Read them, and carefully note your gut-level reactions.

Advantages
  a. You are the boss.
  b. You will have a high degree of control.
  c. You can benefit from tax advantages. [Because of deducting part of home expenses for home office, for example.]
  d. You have the potential for higher earnings. [No limit set by anyone else.]
  e. You enjoy self-fulfillment.
  f. You can create your own work environment.
  g. You have less stress.
  h. You can save money. [On rents, commuting expense, wardrobe]
  i. You have more time with your family.
  j. You can have flexible working hours.

Great, huh? When do we start? Well, before you do anything drastic, read Sheedy's next list:

Disadvantages
  a. There will be monetary risk.
  b. There will be pressure to perform.
  c. You will need to be an expert in a variety of tasks.
  d. It may be difficult to leave work behind.
  e. There is the possibility of irregular income.
  f. You will face loneliness and isolation.
  g. You might have motivation difficulties.
  h. Business may stay with you after hours. [Customers assume you're always available.][2]

Some people couldn't live with even one of those eight disadvantages. Some won't understand how advantage "g" (less stress) can possibly coexist with disadvantages "a" and "e" (monetary risk and irregular income). Those people will never survive self-employment, and they have probably stopped reading this and gone on to the next chapter.

Work Habits Don't Change

If you're still reading, self-employment probably appeals to you. How can you tell if you're prepared to go to work for yourself? One reliable clue is the way you worked when you worked for somebody else. Take a good look at your work habits and ask "Would I want to hire myself as an unsupervised employee?" Your work patterns aren't likely to change for the better when you don't have a supervisor to check up on you. For example:

☐ Do you like to initiate things, or do you wait for someone else to tell you what to do?

☐ Can you figure out how to do things, or do you need clear step-by-step instructions from an authority?

☐ Do you enjoy solving problems as they arise, or do you prefer to let someone else solve them?

☐ Do you enjoy variety, or do you like the security of a set routine?

Unless you are a self-starter who enjoys the challenge of solving every problem that comes up, it's probably better for you to continue looking for "regular" employment.

One self-employed person found that his most valuable training came from doing time in state prison. He's P. J. Estep, a prisoner in the Colorado Correctional System for sixteen years. ("Sixteen years, two months and two days" to be exact.) Estep learned computers in prison, and when he got out, he started two computer businesses—a publishing company putting out technical manuals, and a software consulting business.

As an ex-convict, Estep had no driver's license and no credit, and his reputation followed him to the bank. On the positive side, he found several ways prison had prepared him for self-employment:

One advantage is that *I am used to doing without.* This can be a major advantage in starting a business, since few entrepreneurs can afford everything they would like to have. . . .

Perhaps the biggest advantage I have is that *I do not have high expectations.* . . . Since my experience for the last sixteen years has been that nothing worked the way I had planned, I don't get as frustrated when checks do not arrive when promised, or when the printer doesn't deliver on time.

In prison, you learn to do one day at a time. Owning your own business should be approached in the same way. Take on problems when they arise, handle them in the best way you can, and go on.[3] (emphasis added)

Beware of Scams

Caution: there are a lot of "work-at-home" scams out there. Perhaps the most crafty is the full-page magazine ad promising to sell you the secret method of making a fortune. (It always shows happy people standing in front of a big house and new car.) "No effort," they say. "Just sit back and watch the money roll in," they say. If you send in the money they ask for, you get instructions for putting ads in magazines—ads like the one you just fell for.

Lyn says she wasted about $400 on ads of that type and the "stuff-envelopes-at-home" type before she wised up. (She never got paid for all her envelope stuffing because they claimed she didn't do it exactly according to instructions.) Don't pursue any offer that asks you to send in money for "further information."

There is reliable self-employment information you can pursue at no cost. Go back to your library and look for publications aimed at self-employed people. In our own library we found a couple dozen books on working for yourself (see the Suggested Reading). Our phone company, Wisconsin Bell, offers a free newsletter called *Work at Home.* Though it's a thinly disguised ad for increased phone service, it always has some helpful hint or interesting story.

Look specifically for books and magazines that target people working in the field you want to work. There are a lot of esoteric publications out there. For example, the article by the former prisoner was in *Midnight Engineering,* a magazine aimed at computer hackers who market their own systems and software. We often consult *Writer's Market,* an annual catalog of publishers who accept freelance work.

Yes, I Am Working

A woman who works at home in something other than homemaking will find it difficult to be taken seriously—she's just pursuing a hobby. A man who works at home will be suspected of having something less than a real job—or even being less than a real person. You'll find that support (even a little) helps a lot. You don't have to be surrounded by other self-employed people, but you need some people who believe that you really do have an honest-to-goodness job.

Bret used to work at home as a freelance artist. His wife was also an artist but was employed at a business in town. The phone often rang with salespeople—vacuum cleaners, light bulbs, household items, and so forth—all asking to talk to "the lady of the house."

"Well," Bret would say, "she's not here. You can talk to me."

"Well, I really prefer to talk to your wife."

"But I'm here and she's not," Bret would protest, "and I do a lot of the cooking and shopping. What do you want to tell me?" Usually, the salesperson was very uncomfortable talking with a man at home. Bret eventually moved to his own studio, where he now has the appearance of a "real" workplace—though his work hasn't changed at all.

Mark Off Your Space

If you are working at home, clearly delineate a work space separate from your living space. The mental separation may be as important as the physical. Since not every home willingly yields up such space, it may take some time and experimenting.

When we bought our current home, only one room logically presented itself as an office—an open area at the top of the stairs, which the bedroom opens onto. It works well because it's spacious and well heated, has a nice view from the window and because not one piece of paper ever crosses the threshold to the bedroom.

You need to delineate your work space for several reasons. First, your work at home will take over enormous amounts of your time and conversation. Have mercy on yourself and your family by not letting work take over your living space as well.

Second, setting aside a home office space announces to your family, yourself and others that you're serious. This is a business and not a kitchen-table hobby.

Third, you need to keep certain things and people out of your work space. One market researcher who works from his home had trouble with his answering machine till he realized his cat liked to curl up on the warm device, making it garble messages.[4] Curious children's fingers on a computer disk can wipe out weeks of work.

Fourth, you may be able to deduct the cost of your home office from your federal income taxes. The IRS is very fussy about home offices, so check the latest tax laws. A desk in the corner of your spare bedroom does not qualify as a "home office" for IRS purposes, no matter how well it serves that purpose for you.

How High-Tech?

Most people who start their own businesses immediately think of putting everything on computer. Salespeople stand eager to sell you the most powerful model available, but that's not your first consideration. A homeworking couple give five basic steps for computerizing your home office:

1. Know what you need a computer to do.

2. Locate the software you need.
3. Find the right computer hardware.
4. Get the service and support you need to use your computer.
5. Stay within your budget.[5]

Besides computers, there is a smorgasbord of modern communications technology from faxes to phone mail. It all helps keep you in touch with the outside world, and prices are coming down all the time; but don't succumb to the idea that your business has to acquire every new gadget.

Our own home office is rather low-tech: an "obsolete" computer, a low-cost writing program, a secondhand typewriter, and a vintage phone from the 1940s. We mail in manuscripts on disk as well as in printed form, but we don't have a phone modem because it's seldom necessary to get things to a publisher instantaneously.

What Image?

As you start to assemble your advertising, letterhead, business cards and so forth, think very carefully about the image you want to project—that is, how do you want people to perceive your business? Folksy? Pizzazzy? Elegant? High-tech? Down-to-earth? Design and draw your own logo only if you have artistic talent or you want a "homemade" look. It pays to take your basic concept to a professional artist rather than project an amateurish image.

When people see your mailing address in print, what image does it call to mind? Sandy has never liked having a street address that's a number instead of a name. A writer's address isn't all that important, but if you are selling body-building equipment and you live on Pansy Lane, you might want to consider a post office box or some other option. (However, post office box numbers as a sole address can make your business look fly-by-night.)

Would You Make a Good Employer?

If your business prospers, and you and your family can no longer do all the work yourselves, will you be ready to hire employees? Are you good at giving orders graciously? Can you clearly explain the work you expect your employees to do? Will you give them the freedom to take responsibility to do their work well?

Dale did some carpentry work for a man who was not secure enough to trust anyone to do any work. He would show him exactly what he wanted—and then he would go ahead and do it. Dale got paid to watch him do most of the work! Physically, it made the days easier; emotionally, Dale felt that his boss thought he was incompetent.

Have You Thought About Why?

Now before you start remodelling the rec room and putting in another phone line, wait. Have you examined the reasons you are attracted by the idea of starting your own business?

Do you believe you can offer a better service or product than is already available? Do you want to create your own work life rather than accept someone else's definition of it? Do you feel the need for personal development and challenge?

Our artist-friend Bret has a T-shirt with the message: "Say No to Real Jobs." Working for yourself can open the door to freer and more flexible living. But anybody who thinks it means "saying no to real work" is mistaken.

If you decide to go into business for yourself, be sure you know what you want to do and be willing to take risks. Don't expect to get rich overnight or sit back and watch your business grow on its own. Be prepared to work long and hard hours, experience disappointments, and challenge yourself to the limits.[6]

The literal meaning of *entrepreneur* is "one who undertakes a task," and it is a task to start one's own business. If by escaping the normal workplace you expect to escape pressure and problems, self-employment will disappoint you. Richard K. Irish, who runs his own consulting firm for job-hunting executives, cautions, "Don't think you will be independent. You'll be more dependent than ever on the need for business."[7]

The Iffiness of Cash
If you become self-employed, do something you can do for the love of it as well as for the money, because your cash flow is going to be iffy. "If your primary goal is to make money," says a woodworker named David Orth, "your joy is going to suffer."

David should know. It took him years to seriously consider woodworking as a vocation because he never saw it as a way to make a living. Once he allowed himself to pursue the work that he loved, he found that he could make a living—a modest living, but a living. Enough of a living to enable him to continue loving his work.[8]

Remember, where you once relied on a regular salary, you will now be completely dependent on people paying up what they owe you. That leads to absurd inconsistencies between income and outgo. It also renders the question "Are we making it?" hard to answer.

Jack Stockman, a freelance illustrator, has found himself in the illogical position of doing thousands of dollars' worth of work and still having to borrow money for basic living.

"I might have $20,000 worth of outstanding billings at any given time that I can't bill until I finish an entire project," Jack explains. "And even after I bill a client, it may be sixty to ninety days before I get paid. So that's why my wife and I had to borrow money from a friend to pay the rent this month. We hated doing it, but we had no choice."[9]

The cash-flow situation does have a happier side. When the $20,000 (or a substantial part of it) does come in, you can comfortably endure a subsequent time of no income. We have gone for several months with no income at all but could survive because of a substantial lump-sum payment that already came in.

The Worst Reasons—But They Worked

We did not go into writing to get rich quick. (That's lucky, because we have not gotten rich—even slowly.) We went into writing full-time for probably the worst reasons in the world. Sandy had been doing some curriculum writing while Dale was searching for a job as a Christian education director in a church (and doing handyman work). Dale helped with some writing assignments, and more and more things were starting to carry both of our bylines. Meanwhile the Christian-education job search kept looking promising and then falling through.

Sitting on the edge of our bed, after one particularly frustrating job interview, over ten years ago, Dale asked Sandy, "Why don't we forget about it and just go write?"

That is probably one of the worst reasons for going into business on your own: because you give up in disgust over nothing else working. Possibly it would never have worked for us, except that:

1. we had already published for pay;
2. we knew we were capable of doing the work we expected to make a living doing;
3. we had low expectations of physical comforts and conveniences;
4. we were willing and able to relocate in a depressed area where housing is cheap;
5. the work could be done via mail from anywhere;
6. we were committed to one another;
7. we already had years of experience with Dale's self-employment as a handyman.

(That last point raises a question we've never thought of before: why aren't we counting the beginning of Dale's handyman self-employment as the time we went into self-employment? Probably because he kind of fell into that, and we always regarded it as "temporary fill-in" rather than a business to which we were committed.)

We hope your reasons for becoming self-employed are better than ours. Remember, though, that even our less-than-perfect reasons got us where we were supposed to be. Though it did not seem like a "call" at the time—it seemed like the only workable option—God used that circumstance to call us into a particular kind of work.

Seeing Needs and Doing Something

Probably the most dominant reason for going into self-employment is the appeal of being your own boss. If you have had ogres and trolls for bosses, the idea of replacing them with yourself is very attractive. However, if we go back to the vision of the preceding chapter on underemployment, we'll realize that for a Christian there is no such thing as being your own boss. Remember the Scripture from Colossians which says we are serving the Lord and not other people? Changing the boss from somebody else to myself doesn't eliminate the truth that I am really working for the Lord.

If a person establishes or invents a business to serve the Lord, no matter what else it does, it will be involved meeting human needs with compassion. Self-employment may be the ideal opportunity to tailor-make a career to a need you have seen in your world.

The enterprising woman in Proverbs 31 is a wife "of noble character" who "fears the LORD" (vv. 10, 30). She is not only taking care of her household, she is working for financial gain:

She considers a field and buys it;
out of her earnings she plants a vineyard. . . .
She sees that her trading is profitable,
and her lamp does not go out at night. . . .
She makes linen garments and sells them,

and supplies the merchants with sashes.
(Proverbs 31:16, 18, 24)

This woman is engaged in a great variety of work, and though she is making money from it, it is not self-centered. In the course of her work she serves the needs of many people.

She opens her arms to the poor
and extends her hands to the needy.
When it snows, she has no fear for her household;
for all of them are clothed in scarlet. . . .
She speaks with wisdom,
and faithful instruction is on her tongue. (31:20-21, 26)

Here is a whole new way of "looking for work": beginning with what others need rather than the job I need! New Horizons North, the business we told you about in the preceding chapter, was started to respond to the obvious needs of specific people: developmentally disabled adults who were too old for school. In the drive for profit, most entrepreneurs don't give much thought to establishing their shops to serve people in need. They may create a consumer demand, but that's not meeting a need. Looking with different eyes, which are really the eyes of Christ, we'll see all kinds of opportunities that Job Service never told us about.

Remember all your dreams and skills we explored in chapter five? Keep them in mind as you explore the human needs that remain unmet in your own community—or even some other place in the world.

Just as in hunting for a regular job, the first step is to search for information. What are the needs around you? What efforts are other people making to do something about them? Or are those needs being ignored? What hasn't worked in the past? Why not? Who else could you interest in trying to meet those needs?

Go Ahead and Try
If self-employment still appeals to you, and if the Lord seems

to be opening things in that direction, why not go ahead and try? Even if your business doesn't succeed as a full-time operation, it can persist as a lucrative and fun part-time job. Even if it folds, it was an interesting and educational experience—as long as it doesn't leave you too deeply in debt.

Helen K. Hosier suggests several reasons not every entrepreneur survives:

☐ The stress and pressures of keeping the venture going.

☐ Insufficient discipline to stick at it.

☐ Inability to manage people and/or don't like the responsibility of handling employees.

☐ Uncomfortable with allowing the employees to be the stars; too accustomed to being in the limelight.

☐ They are not sellers; they are doers. Marketing themselves, their business or service, makes them uncomfortable.

☐ Inability to handle the financial aspects.

☐ No workable business plan to begin with, and/or a plan that may have been good, but wasn't realistic or didn't come up to projections and expectations.[10]

Take those as warnings but don't necessarily let them scare you off. You may be just the person to carve out a career for yourself in cooperation with the Lord.

Things to Do

☐ Talk to all the self-employed people you know and find out what keeps them going.

☐ Talk to all the formerly self-employed people you know and try to determine why the experiment didn't work.

☐ Examine your working habits and ask if you would want to hire yourself as an unsupervised employee.

☐ Identify needs that no one is meeting, and come up with as many creative possibilities as you can for meeting those needs.

☐ Go over the "needs-meeting" list you just made, and imagine how you could put yourself to work at any of them.

Suggested Reading

Edwards, Paul and Sarah. *Working from Home.* Los Angeles: Jeremy P. Tarcher Inc., 1985. The most comprehensive book we found on running a home-based business (though some of its computer information is outdated). Warmly written by a couple who began working from their home in the mid-1970s.

Hosier, Helen K. *Suddenly Unemployed.* San Bernardino, Calif.: Here's Life, 1992. After being recruited for a ministry management position and moved cross-country, Hosier lost her job. In this book she tells how to take charge of such a situation while depending on the Lord.

Internal Revenue Service Publication 334: *Tax Guide for Small Business* and Publication 587: *Business Use of Your Home.*

Kamoroff, Bernard. *Small-Time Operator.* Laytonville, Calif.: Bell Springs Publishing. Revised and updated yearly. Practical (and amusing) workbook for building a business around your interests. Written by a CPA; especially good financial section. Includes a year's worth of ledgers and worksheets.

Karlson, David. *Consulting for Success: A Guide for Prospective Consultants.* Los Altos, Calif.: Crisp Publications, 1991. Workbook format for becoming an independent consultant, selling your skills on a contract basis—including to your own former employer!

Kern, Coralee Smith, and Tammara Hoffman Wolfgram. *How to Run Your Own Home Business.* Lincolnwood, Ill.: VGM Career Horizons, 1990. Deciding if you're suited to working at home, how to select a business, set up, daily operation of service and product businesses, and current trends. Many worksheets.

Sheedy, Edna. *Start and Run a Profitable Home-Based Business.* Bellingham, Wash.: Self-Counsel Press, 1990. Lots of practical help on setting up a business in your home and keeping it going.

9

Helping
Each Other

You know the other person is struggling,
and you don't have the magic word for the moment—
but we're in this marriage and we're dealing with this together.
But you don't always feel real together.
Susan, on her husband Tom's unemployment

Therefore encourage one another and build each other up,
just as in fact you are doing.
1 Thessalonians 5:11

This chapter is for spouses, friends, church members, anyone who knows and cares about someone out of work. It's also for unemployed people: to help make our expectations of others more realistic; to help us help each other; and to remind us that when we are employed again, we can still reach out to those still out of work.

It Seems We Can't Win
When employed people try to help unemployed people, sometimes everybody winds up frustrated. We're really all in the same communication bind.

When we're unemployed, we want to know that our joblessness matters to somebody besides ourselves. We wait to hear words of encouragement spoken at the right time, but it doesn't happen. People say they care, but it isn't said right—or it's said too often—or it fails to come exactly when we want it—or we detect beneath it a mood of judgment and impatience.

Meanwhile, would-be helpers feel just as frustrated. They really do want to help, but they don't know what to say. Remember when we asked Victor how he coped with people knowing he had lost his job? He said, "Nobody asked about it." Others don't know what to say, but say something anyway.

There is only one perfect helper; everyone else will fall short. We save ourselves some bitter disappointment if we go to Christ to seek mercy and have mercy on the faltering efforts of others.

> For we do not have a high priest who is unable to sympathize with our weaknesses, but we have one who has been tempted in every way, just as we are—yet was without sin. Let us then approach the throne of grace with confidence, so that we may receive mercy and find grace to help us in our time of need. (Hebrews 4:15-16)

When Jesus promised the Holy Spirit, the Counselor or Comforter "to be with you forever" (John 14:16), he knew that human counselors and comforters would not be enough for us.

How Are You? (Don't Tell Me)

After Mary Jo Purcell lost her job, she noticed that people stopped greeting her with the usual innocuous question "How are you?"

"Once I thought the question meaningless, akin to a burp; now it appears to be said, or not said, with forethought. . . . Obviously, friends and acquaintances are either reacting with touching sensitivity or are in utter fear of hearing how I am."[1]

While some people are afraid to ask "How are you?" others may ask it—or some form of it—too much. When Tony lost his job with a travel agency, his wife, Dawn, was employed part-time as a legal aide. Fortunately, she was able to add more hours to her work as the family became completely dependent on her income. Because Tony was well known in town, his unemployment was also well known. Dawn and Tony were—and still are—grateful for people's concern during that difficult time. But Dawn remembers their expressions of concern sometimes causing strain:

> It was so hard being asked all the time, "Has he found anything yet?" You don't know what to say. But I think basically people asked because they cared. I know another woman whose husband is out of work, but it's been a long time since I asked her about it because I remember what it was like to be asked all the time.

Of course, there are such things as "fair-weather friends" who avoid us when we start having problems. We wonder why our joblessness suddenly disqualifies us from their friendship. Their reaction to our job loss may depend on factors that have little to do with us:

- ☐ how threatened they feel by our job loss ("Am I next?")
- ☐ how long we stay out of work ("Hasn't she found anything yet?")
- ☐ how they perceive the circumstances of our job loss ("Well, it was his own fault.")
- ☐ how much is going wrong in their own lives at the moment ("I know it's rough, but I've got my hands full with my own problems right now.")
- ☐ how strong they perceive us to be ("They're doing okay, he's got a lot of skills, he'll find something soon.")

Ironically, some of the people we expected to support us the most may turn out to care the least, and people we barely knew before may turn out to be the most supportive. We save ourselves a lot of grief if we decide (harsh as it sounds) that we can't demand support from other people. We spend enough energy looking for work and being disappointed. Why waste more energy always being on the lookout for sympathy and being disappointed? Giving up the demand for support frees us to find support in surprising places—or to let it find us.

When Your Stomach Churns

Imperfect as we are, we are called to help and comfort and encourage each other as God comforts us (2 Corinthians 1:3-5). How can we do it?

To begin with, when we ask our unemployed friends, "How are you?" or "How are things going?" what do we mean? Do we mean "I want to know the latest and also how you feel" and will we sympathetically listen? Or do we mean "Haven't you found something yet?" or "Why aren't you looking harder?"

You may recall how Kyle described his family's response to his unemployment: "It becomes *the* topic of conversation—'Have you found anything yet? Are you looking?' "

Susan says she appreciates her family's concern about her husband Tom's job search, but sometimes it turns from support into pressure. What's the difference, we asked, between support and pressure? She answered, "When your gut starts to churn then you know it's pressure."

Perhaps a better strategy than asking, "How are things going?" or "Have you found anything yet?" is to tell the person, "I'm thinking of you," or "I'm praying for you." That opens the door for the person to volunteer information. It allows the person to graciously answer, "Thank you" and leave it at that, or to tell you as much as they choose about hopes or disappointments.

Help from the World

Many people suffering through difficulty say they find more support outside the church than inside, and unemployment fits that pattern. While Dale was searching for a Christian education job, and Sandy was working temp secretarial jobs, we attended a good church and got into an excellent Bible study group. Sandy found, however, that when there was a disappointment in the job search, she would get more satisfying responses and support from the people at her current temp job than from people at church.

"He didn't get it? That's terrible! Isn't life crummy?" (and so forth) people in the "outside world" would say. Meanwhile at church he would hear, "Well, the Lord must have something else for you," or "You must be supposed to stay here." Now everything that was said at church was true. Why did it seem less supportive?

The secular sympathy felt more real because it echoed Sandy's own feelings. People let her know they knew how she was feeling; and that was what, in those first moments of conversation, she really needed. The response of the church would have been good for beyond that—after they let her know they knew how she felt.

Christians seem especially prone to easy answers. We believe that Christ is the answer to our problems, and therefore for every problem we expect to have an answer. We want to "fix" the situation or the person right away.

There are blessed exceptions. Remember (from chapter two) how Norm went to church ready to attack the pastor? He recalls, "That man disarmed my hurt by entering into my anger. How are you going to jump on somebody that's on your side of the fence?"

Husbands and Wives

When the unemployed person you care about is your own spouse, you're up against a complex set of circumstances and emotions. You also have a great opportunity to make all the difference in the life of the person you love most.

When Lloyd lost his managerial position, he and his teen-aged family had to start living on his wife Marge's salary as a government supervisor. It meant living on less, but as Lloyd put it, "The emotional is worse than the financial."

He went on, "How do I handle being dependent on Marge financially? I've accepted it without liking it. I'm a traditionalist. It gives me black moods now and then. I know I haven't dealt with it. It hurts."

Lloyd and Marge's unemployment situation—husband out of work, wife working—is very normal today. Typically, the husband has had the better-paying job, and the wife has worked either part-time or full-time at a lower-paying job. When the man's job vanishes, they are left depending on her income. Never mind that we're in an age of equality and loosened sex roles; whether right or wrong, most men still prefer to be the chief provider.

If the wife's becoming sole provider is hard on the husband, it can be hard on the wife too. Dawn found it hard to understand when Tony got "stuck" in his job search. Coming home tired after her legal-aide work, she would be irritated that he hadn't taken as much initiative as she thought he should.

My perception of what he was doing to seek employment was different from his. I'd come home and the house would be a mess, and he'd made a couple of phone calls. I'd think, "I worked eight hours and you made two phone calls?" His perception was "That's all I could do." That's all the energy he could muster.

At a time like that, the impulse of many wives is to take over the whole effort. Therefore, one unemployment support group states this guideline in capital letters: "DO NOT TAKE RESPONSIBILITY FOR ANYONE ELSE'S JOB SEARCH." That's perhaps the biggest temptation of any of us, whether spouses or friends: to try to help too much. We can see exactly what the unemployed person ought to do.

Susan remembers her first flurry of effort after Tom lost his job at a sail-maker's shop:

I tried to encourage him, and maybe I did too much. I was the one who got his résumé going, set up an office space for him in the corner of the dining room, got an extra-long phone cord so it could reach from the kitchen. I thought I was being a good wife by doing all of that, but later I realized, "This is his job. He has to decide what type of work and when and where."

After that initial burst of activity, Susan decided it was wise to pull back a little. "I thought it was more something we would do together," she says, "but I've pulled away from it a little emotionally. Maybe so it wasn't as painful—but also I realized that *he* has to do this." Also it turned out that Tom interpreted some of Susan's help as pushy. She says:

I was working and he was home taking care of our preschool child and making phone contacts. I'd come in the door and start asking what had happened that day. I had this whole other schedule in my mind. I knew who might be calling that day, what interviews were pending, and he didn't always like being grilled about it. I learned to wait on some of that.

Jeannine did not get as involved as Susan in her husband Rolf's job search, but she found much survival value in praying and staying positive. Rolf had worked in a rather obscure branch of scientific research. When its funding was lost, so was his career. She recalls: "My praying centered around that God would support the family every single day. My long-term prayer was that he knew what kind of job Rolf should have. Short-term, it was our financial needs. So God had to be my reliance both short-term and long-term."

Remember from chapter two how Norm quoted his wife, Sylvia, saying things as simple as "I believe in you" or "We'll make it"? Sylvia stayed positive. For Jeannine, part of being positive was to keep busy and to keep Rolf busy. She encouraged him to keep sending out his research résumé—even though prospects in that field were not good.

He had tunnel vision about going back to work in his particular scientific field. I tried to get him to look at a wider range of careers. At the same time I encouraged him to keep sending out his résumés in that field. Even though it was maybe not the right thing to do, if it made him feel better it was the right thing to do.

Ultimately, however, Jeannine knew that Rolf's career was in the hands of the Lord. "I told him he had to wait until the Lord was ready to provide. We had to wait it out together. We were all eating and we were still functioning fine."

Find Something Funny

Jeannine found that a sense of humor was all-important, especially with teenagers in the family. Because she is very upbeat by nature, for her the most stressful part of Rolf's unemployment was his negative moods.

Sometimes I would put him in the same category as a teenager because he was so caught up in himself. I would try and find something light and airy—something we could laugh about. Sometimes he would get so caught up in himself that he wasn't realizing how everything else was working together.

A sense of humor may have to include what the house looks like during certain periods of a job search. Susan has had to learn to trust Tom to do more of the work at home. She says, "I was doing most of the housework as well as working, but at a certain point I said, 'This is all I'm going to do.' It gets pretty bad, but eventually he does it. He's broken a lot of dishes and sometimes we all have pink underwear, but that's part of my pulling back."

Pulling back means letting the other person take responsibility; it does not mean cutting off communication. Somehow, hard as it is sometimes, a husband and wife must keep talking— not only about the details of job prospects but about their feelings and hurts and hopes.

We found that our own relationship deepened and intensified while Dale was looking unsuccessfully for the church job.

Sometimes our own relationship was all we had going for us. Dawn remembers a similar time in her life:

There would be times when I'd want to talk about it, and he wouldn't. I guess I always did want to talk about it all the time. Sometimes our perceptions were different. They were the same when we were both hoping and trying not to hope too hard. Like when we'd think we were moving and we'd get out the map and dream together. Maybe that helps you get through it.

Norm admitted that he couldn't always talk to Sylvia about it all, not because he didn't want to, but because "I haven't known what my emotions were or how to say it."

Susan finds that she and Tom are often "on different emotional planes," but each knows the other is struggling, and they love each other. "Our culture has this image of supporting each other as holding hands before a beautiful sunset," she says. "But maybe you're in separate rooms doing separate things, but you're still supporting and loving each other."

Get Organized

If family and church support aren't enough, or if you feel you need to connect with other unemployed people to help each other's job searches, you may want to find an unemployment support group. If there's none in your area, you may be just the person to get one started, perhaps through your church. Talk to your pastor and others in leadership about the need and your interest and willingness. If they don't see any need, don't be discouraged; you know there's a need, and you may have to go ahead on your own. Ask other unemployed people if they'd be interested. Ask about people who have special skills who could help by giving seminars or leading discussion groups.

Several years ago Central Presbyterian Church in Clayton, Missouri, started a support group for people out of work. John Vasse explains how the ministry grew and changed in response to the needs of the people who walked in the door: "We soon discovered that those who came for 'support' hadn't a clue about how to start or conduct a job search. For most, this was their first experience at being unemployed, and while the emotional and spiritual support was certainly needed, some basic instructional sessions were also needed."

As a result, Central developed a seven-week employment ministry of weekly seminars on subjects such as emotional survival, résumés, interviewing, skills inventory, and alternative careers. Vasse explains:

A committee of about ten or twelve is responsible for running the ministry. As I feel I must point out to everyone, we're a bunch of amateurs. Of course, that's one reason our price is right—zero.

The weekly instructional sessions are offered by members of the committee. Their "expertise" comes from their having been through a job search themselves, plus reading/study: "on the job training" so to speak.

On the same evenings as the seminars, a professional counselor from Central's Christian counseling center is available to talk with seminar attendees or spouses.

Another practical employment ministry of Central Presbyterian is a bulletin board in the church dining room where the names of people seeking employment, and the employment they are seeking, are posted on 3 x 5 cards. The congregation is asked to let the church know of job openings they're aware of at their own places of employment, and those are posted on cards on the same bulletin board.

The job search support group at Westminster Presbyterian Church in Wilmington, Delaware, has been meeting since April 1991. Robert Bryant states their three objectives:

1. Provide emotional support during job search/career reviews.
2. Develop job search objectives, plans, tools and skills.

3. Cultivate networking contacts.

For getting started, Westminster says "a committed facilitator" is "essential." "Highly desirable" are "another committed facilitator" and "that at least one of the facilitators has experience job searching." "Helpful" are a "regular meeting place" and "job search materials."

Support Group Guidelines
In slightly condensed form, here are Westminster's guidelines for the support group leader:

1. Create a safe haven, where people can speak in confidence without fear of criticism or judgments.
2. Remain upbeat and positive in attitude within the bounds of being "real." Accept and legitimize people's natural feelings resulting from job loss, but also help people focus on the future.
3. People help themselves enormously by helping others. The principal effort at a meeting could be to focus the whole group on a single person's needs for that week.
4. There is no single "right" way to find a job. Each seeker must develop a career objective and a search plan which fits his or her unique set of abilities, interests and style of selling him/herself.
5. DO NOT TAKE RESPONSIBILITY FOR ANYONE ELSE'S JOB SEARCH.
6. Visit some established groups. Try out their tools, materials, procedures.
7. Develop weekly agendas and policies regarding speakers and participants as a group.
8. Two hours is a good regular meeting length. Subgroups can meet separately for special tasks.
9. Eight to twelve is a good meeting size. If the group is consistently larger, consider splitting into two groups.
10. Participants must be candid with each other to help each

other. Candidness is constructive only after mutual trust is established.

11. Spouses of the job seekers need support at least as much as the seekers. They can feel even more out of control, since they cannot take direct action to find the job both depend upon. A separate support group for spouses can be helpful.

Here is Westminster's suggested meeting format:

1. Sign in. (The sign-in sheet is copied and distributed to those attending to help people contact each other for help.)
2. Prayer/inspiration.
3. Reminder of confidentiality of everything discussed.
4. Self-introductions by everyone to each other:
   □ "2 minute drill." (Who you are professionally, what you've done, what you want to do.)
   □ Weekly goals and whether they were met. (If someone's goal was simply to get to the support group meeting that week and he got there, he achieved his weekly goals. People must set their own goals.)
   □ Good news. (Sometimes the only good news is that the house did not burn down.)
   □ Special needs this week.
5. Help each other with special needs.
6. Guest speaker/facilitator. (Every other week maximum; otherwise there is not enough time together to help each other.)
7. Discuss future meeting agendas.

Spouses Need Support

Dawn recalls feeling trapped when people came to her to advise her about what Tony should be doing. "That caught me in the middle because I couldn't do anything about it. I was doing stuff but he wasn't, so why were they talking to me?"

Newsweek's financial columnist Jane Bryant Quinn (whose brother Robert leads the Westminster Presbyterian group) notes that "almost no research has been done on the spouses of the unemployed. They feel the same shame, fear and loss of control that the job seeker does, yet they're powerless to end their trials."[2]

Don't forget the spouse. And don't forget the children. A little note or gift, however small, can make all the difference in a day of unemployment.

If You've Got the Right Suit?

No matter how much we want to help or be helped, in the end there is only one recourse for help. If unemployment drives us to that recourse, it has done a good work in us no matter what else happens. Dawn says that she and Tony found their sense of certainty shifting from job to Christ:

I'm an organized person who likes to have my lists and my calendar, and I didn't even know what state we were moving to. I came to a growing realization that the certainty is with Christ and not with employment. Gradually we went from "If you've got the right suit and your résumé is good and you make enough calls, you'll get the job" to "If God opens the door . . ."

Having a meaningful job that pays well is a good thing. It is not the only thing. It is not even the best thing. A job does not make life perfect because work and workers have all been flawed since humanity left the Garden.

There will be unemployed people who find satisfying careers; there will be those who get their dream jobs and are disappointed; there will be some who have to settle for less than they had before; and there will be others who find joy in unexpected roles and places.

When we don't even know how to pray for ourselves or our families, "the Spirit himself intercedes for us with groans that words cannot express" (Romans 8:26). God has plans for each of us. We pray that everyone reading this book will find meaningful work, but even more than that, that your relationship with Christ will be deepened through this experience.

Things for the Unemployed to Do
☐ Keep talking with your spouse.
☐ Consider starting or joining a support group.
☐ Keep a sense of humor.
· ☐ Thank people for their concern even if they don't express it as you'd like.
☐ Remember, only Christ is the perfect helper.

Things for Helpers to Do
☐ Refrain from trying to "fix" the person or the situation.
☐ Before you ask how things are, consider whether you're expressing concern or trying to elicit a particular answer.
☐ State your care and concern, then leave it open for the unemployed person to respond, rather than asking questions which the person may not know how to answer.
☐ Remember the spouse and children.

Notes

Chapter One: Not Just a Victim
[1]Robert Coulson, *The Termination Handbook* (New York, N.Y.: The Free Press, 1981), p. 27.
[2]Ibid., p. 4.
[3]Bonnie Angelo, "Life at the End of the Rainbow," *Time*, November 4, 1991, p. 80.
[4]Jon Tevlin, "Big Winners," *Minnesota Monthly*, February 1992, p. 60.
[5]Coulson, *Termination*, p. 16.

Chapter Two: Getting Unstuck: Reclaiming Control
[1]Paula Leventman, *Professionals out of Work* (New York, N.Y.: The Free Press, 1981), p. 148.
[2]Coulson, *Termination*, p. 19.
[3]John E. I. Ogar, "While I Wait," *Decision*, July-August 1992, p. 36.
[4]Tim Hansel, *You Gotta Keep Dancin'* (Elgin, Ill.: David C. Cook, 1985), p. 37.
[5]Ray Hyman and Barry Anderson, "Solve It," *Chemtech*, May 1980, pp. 276-78. Originally published in *International Science and Technology*.
[6]Maurice Wagner, *The Sensation of Being Somebody* (Grand Rapids, Mich.: Zondervan, 1975), p. 162.
[7]Ronald L. Krannich, *Careering and Re-careering for the 1990s* (Manassas, Va.: Impact, 1989), p. 114.
[8]Harry Maurer, *Not Working: An Oral History of the Unemployed* (New York, N.Y.: Holt, Rinehart & Winston, 1979), p. 6.

Chapter Three: Buying Time
[1]Richard D. Perry, *Money Problems* (Elgin, Ill.: David C. Cook, 1987), p. 14.
[2]Robert Half, *How to Get a Better Job in This Crazy World* (New York, N.Y.: Crown, 1990), p. 94.
[3]Howard Figler, *The Complete Job-Search Handbook: All the Skills You Need to Get Any Job and Have a Good Time Doing It*, rev. ed. (New York, N.Y.: Henry Holt, 1988), p. 222.
[4]Ibid., p. 212.
[5]Ibid., p. 224.

Chapter Five: What Do You Really Want?
[1]John C. Crystal and Richard N. Bolles, *Where Do I Go from Here with My Life?* (Berkeley, Calif.: Ten Speed Press, 1974), p. 31.
[2]Richard K. Irish, *Go Hire Yourself an Employer*, rev. ed. (New York, N.Y.: Anchor Press/Doubleday, 1987), p. xiii.
[3]Janis Long Harris, *Secrets of People Who Love Their Work* (Downers Grove, Ill.: InterVarsity Press, 1992), p. 35.
[4]"99 Idea Killers. Beware! They Can Eat You Alive!" (Rapp & Collins, Innovation Labs, Inc., 1980).
[5]"Snack Food Pioneer Dies," *Daily Press,* June 6, 1992.
[6]Irish, *Go Hire,* p. 55.
[7]Ibid., p. 56.
[8]Figler, *Complete,* p. 62.
[9]Krannich, *Careering,* p. 126.
[10]Suzanne Seixas, "Santa in the Red," *Money,* December 1990, pp. 122-29.
[11]Frank Lalli, "How to be Rich in America Today," *Money,* December 1990, p. 7.
[12]Krannich, *Careering,* p. 87.
[13]Amy Saltzman, Mary Lord and Edward C. Baig, "Voices from the Front," *U.S. News & World Report,* January 13, 1992, p. 51.
[14]George Will, "The Cold War Among Women," *Newsweek,* June 26, 1978, p. 100.
[15]Gary Hardway, "When Dreams Die," *Moody Monthly,* June 1986, pp. 19-21.

Chapter Six: Beyond the End of Your Rope: A Guide to Other Resources
[1]Elisabeth Elliot, *A Slow and Certain Light* (Waco, Tex.: Word, 1973), pp. 19-20.
[2]Figler, *Complete,* p. 17.
[3]Ibid., pp. 135-38.

[4]Ibid., p. 124.

[5]Robert Wegmann, Robert Chapman and Miriam Johnson, *Work in the New Economy,* rev. ed. (Indianapolis, Ind.: JIST Works, 1990), p. 93.

[6]Ronald L. Krannich and Caryl Rae Krannich, *Network Your Way to Job & Career Success* (Manassas, Va.: Impact, 1989), pp. 11-12.

[7]Suzanne Seixas, "Laid Off," *Money,* February 1991, p. 86.

[8]Robert Wegmann and Robert Chapman, *The Right Place at the Right Time* (Berkeley, Calif.: Ten Speed Press, 1990), p. 126.

[9]Figler, *Complete,* p. 126.

[10]Richard N. Bolles, *What Color Is Your Parachute?* rev. ed. (Berkeley, Calif.: Ten Speed Press, 1991), p. 147.

[11]Ronald L. Krannich and Caryl Rae Krannich, *Dynamite Cover Letters & Other Great Job Search Letters* (Woodbridge, Va.: Impact, 1992), p. 96.

[12]Bolles, *Parachute,* pp. 160-61.

[13]Figler, *Complete,* pp. 233-44.

[14]Ibid., p. 210.

Chapter Seven: Making the Best of Underemployment

[1]B. H. Throckmorton Jr., "Tentmaker," *Interpreter's Dictionary of the Bible* (Nashville, Tenn.: Abingdon Press, 1962), p. 573.

[2]E. P. Blair, "Gamaliel," *Interpreter's,* p. 351.

[3]W. E. Vine, *An Expository Dictionary of New Testament Words* (London: Oliphants Ltd., 1940), 1:65.

[4]Jerry and Mary White, *Your Job: Survival or Satisfaction? Christian Discipleship in a Secular Job* (Grand Rapids, Mich.: Zondervan, 1977), p. 143.

[5]Ben Patterson, *Work* (Downers Grove, Ill.: InterVarsity Press, 1992). Adapted from chapters 1-4 of *The Grand Essentials* (Waco, Tex.: Word, 1987), pp. 20-21.

Chapter Eight: Making Your Own Way

[1]Thomas McCarroll, "Entrepreneurs: Starting Over," *Time,* January 6, 1992, pp. 62.

[2]Edna Sheedy, *How to Start and Run a Profitable Home-Based Business* (Bellingham, Wash.: Self-Counsel Press, 1990), pp. 1-3.

[3]P. J. Estep, "Getting Out," *Midnight Engineering,* March-April 1991, p. 6.

[4]John Schwartz, Dody Tsiantar and Karen Springen, "Escape from the Office," *Newsweek,* April 24, 1989, p. 59.

[5]Paul and Sarah Edwards, *Working from Home* (Los Angeles: Jeremy P. Tarcher, Inc., 1985), pp. 313-15.

⁶Krannich, *Careering*, p. 271.
⁷Irish, *Go Hire*, p. 16.
⁸Harris, *Secrets*, p. 100.
⁹Ibid., p. 95.
¹⁰Helen K. Hosier, *Suddenly Unemployed* (San Bernardino, Calif.: Here's Life, 1992), pp. 240-41.

Chapter Nine: Helping Each Other
¹Mary Jo Purcell, "Really, I'm Fine—Just Ask Me," *Newsweek*, November 30, 1992, p. 12.
²Jane Bryant Quinn, "Self-Help for the Jobless," *Newsweek*, December 16, 1991, p. 52.